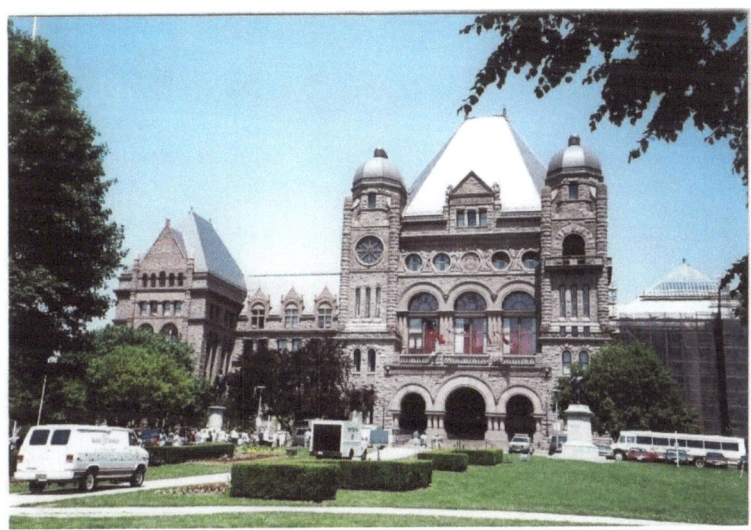

Queen's Park – In 1859 the city leased land from King's College and in 1860 a park named after Queen Victoria was opened by the Prince of Wales. The main block of the massive Romanesque Revival Parliament Buildings with its towering legislative block was completed in 1892.

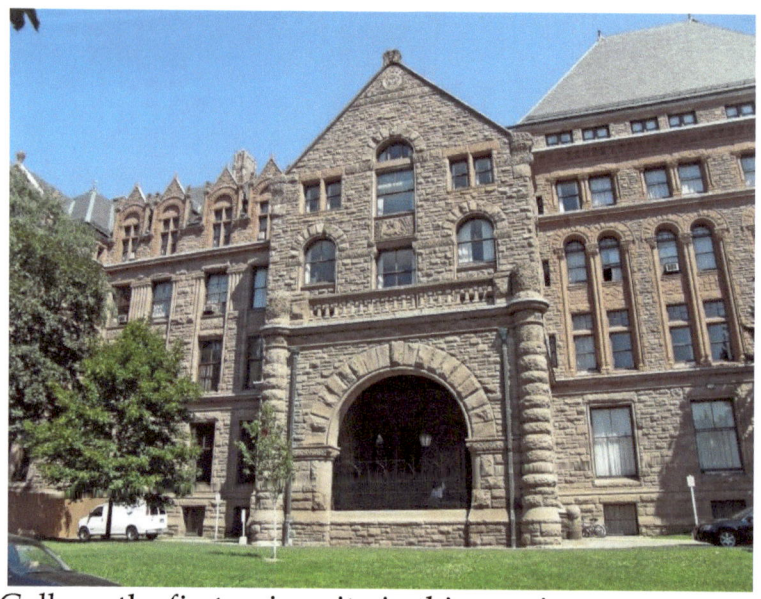

King's College, the first university in this province was chartered in 1827 but it wasn't until 1843 that classes began in the former Parliament Buildings on Front Street. Construction was completed in 1845. King's College offered instruction in the arts, science, law, theology and medicine. In 1850 it became the new University of Toronto.

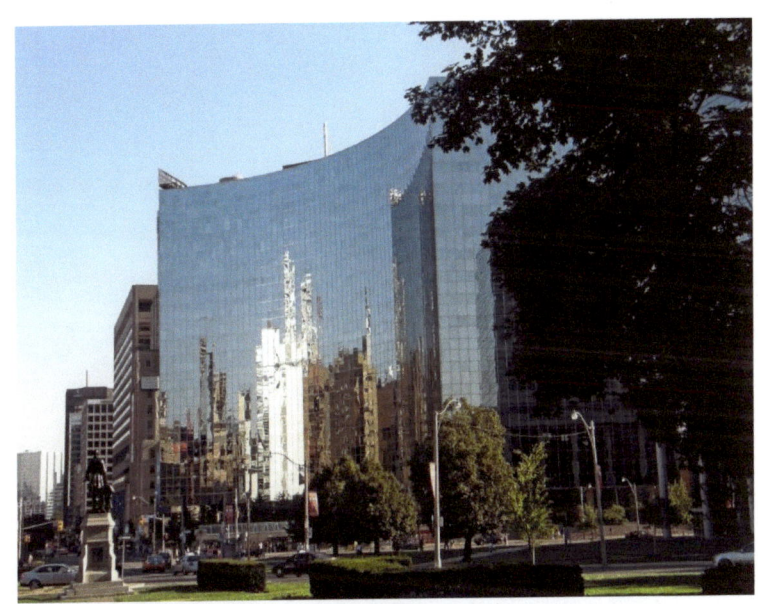

Reflections

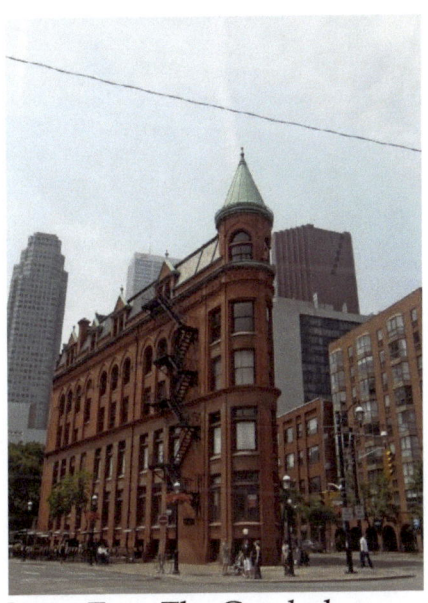

49 Wellington Street East, The Gooderham or Flatiron Building - Romanesque Revival and French Gothic architecture styles - opened in 1892

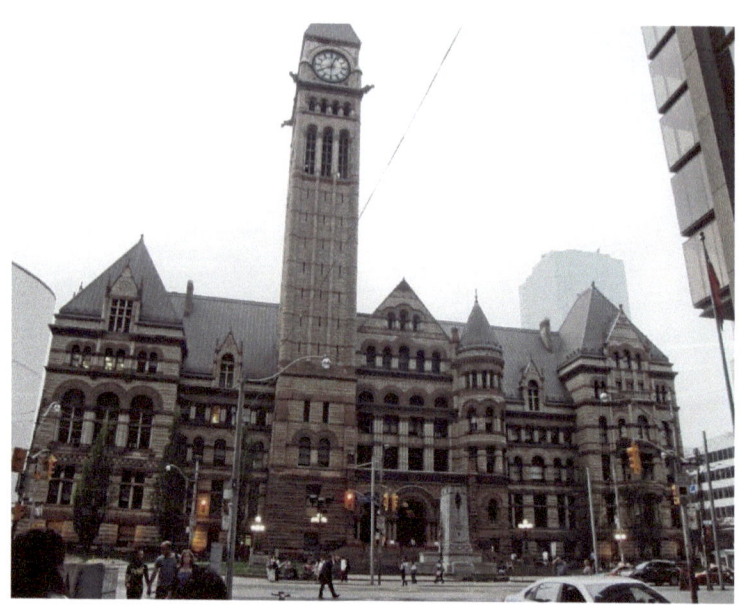
Armouries

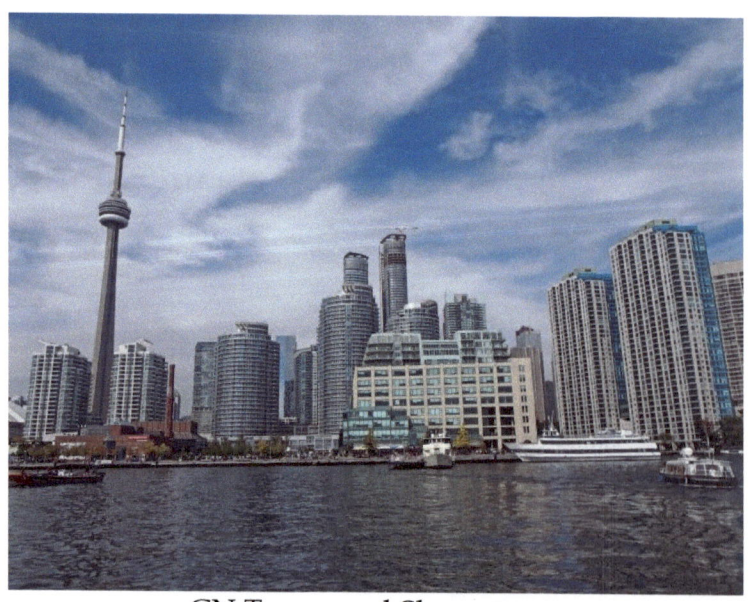
CN Tower and Skyscrapers

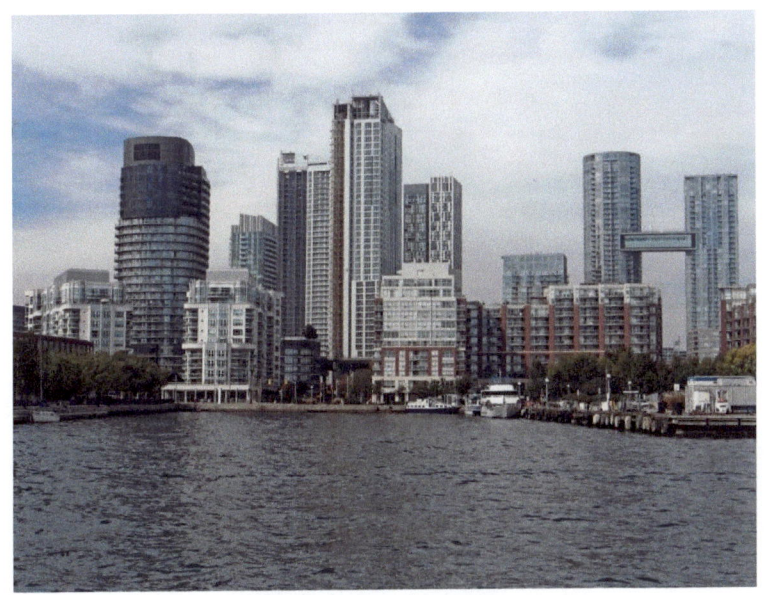

View from the water

Collingwood, Ontario – My Top 9 Picks

Collingwood is situated on Nottawasaga Bay at the southern point of Georgian Bay. Collingwood offers a combination of old time charm and history with recreation opportunities for skiing on Blue Mountain, and golfing.

Collingwood was incorporated as a town in 1858, nine years before Confederation and was named after Admiral Lord Cuthbert Collingwood, Lord Nelson's second in command at the Battle of Trafalgar, who assumed command of the British fleet after Nelson's death.

The land in the area was originally inhabited by the Iroquoian Petun nation, which built a string of villages in the vicinity of the nearby Niagara Escarpment. They were driven from the region by the Iroquois in 1650. European settlers and freed black slaves arrived in the area in the 1840s, bringing with them their religion and culture.

In 1855, the Ontario, Simcoe & Huron (later called The Northern) railway came into Collingwood, and the harbor became the place for shipment of goods destined for the upper Great Lakes ports of Chicago and Port Arthur-Ft. William (now Thunder Bay). Shipping produced a need for ship repairs, so it was not long before an organized ship building business was created. On May 24, 1883, the Collingwood Shipyards, formerly known as Collingwood Dry Dock Shipbuilding and Foundry Company Limited, opened with a special ceremony. On September 12, 1901, the Huronic was launched in Collingwood, the first steel-hulled ship launched in Canada. The shipyards produced Lakers and during World War II contributed to the production of Corvettes for the Royal Canadian Navy.

I couldn't leave out showing you the fiddler on the roof at 296 Pine Street.

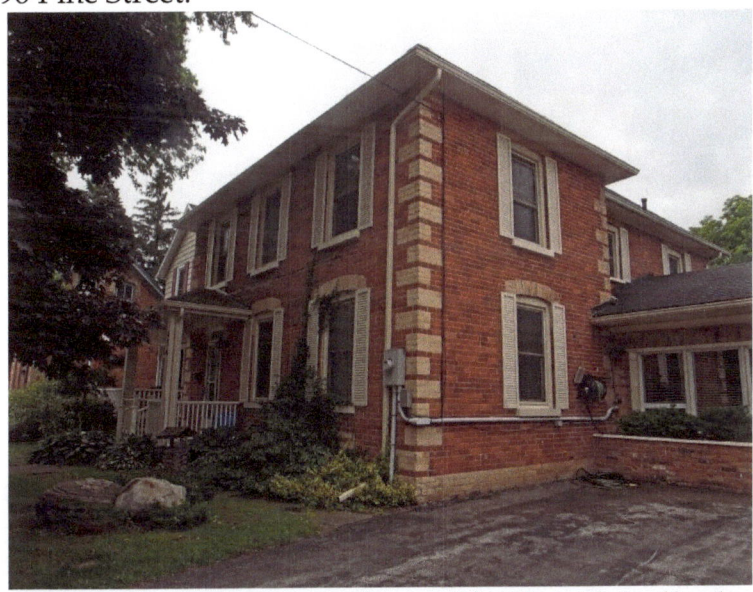

296 Pine Street – Italianate style – red brick with buff coloured accents

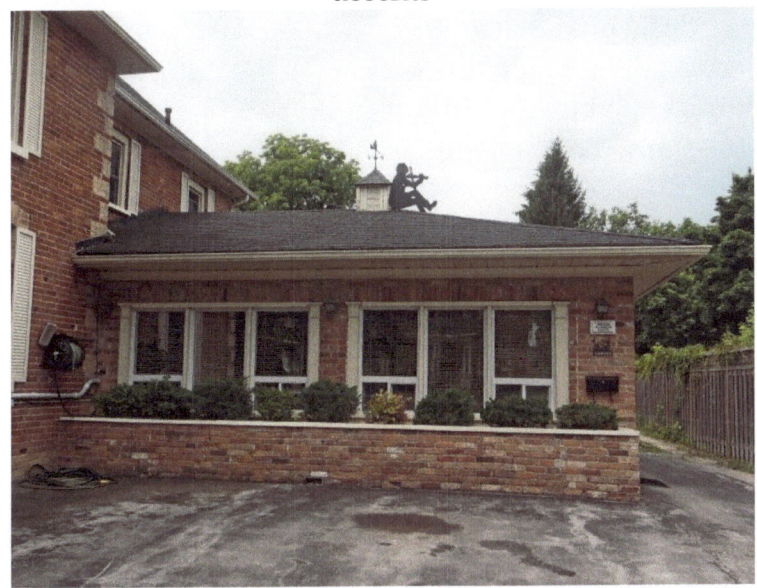

One storey wing with fiddler on the roof - The first date Harry and I went on was to see "Fiddler on the Roof"

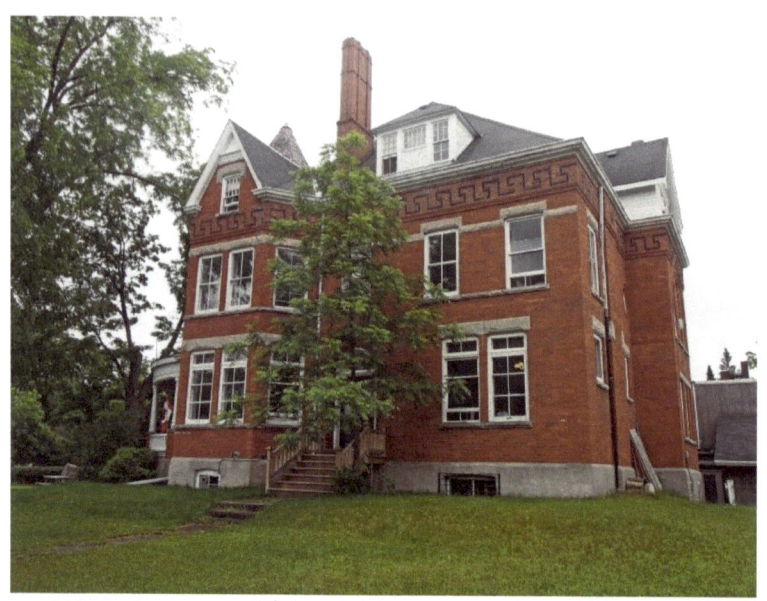

200 Oak Street - This 10,380 square foot Victorian home, the largest and tallest in Collingwood, at the corner of Oak and Third Streets was originally owned by Frank F. Telfer, a leading businessman and ex-mayor of Collingwood. He purchased the property in 1891, and by 1893 the local firm Bryan Brothers Manufacturing Company completed the construction of the Telfer home. In 1925 the Telfer family sold the house, and the "Gowans Home for Missionaries' Children" was established by the Interior Sudan Mission.

This home displays a variety of architectural features. The three storey structure is of double brick construction laid in a stretcher bond fashion and rests on a cut stone foundation. The three main exterior walls are accented by a repeating Greek style pattern running the full width of the walls below the eaves. The northeast corner of the building is formed by a large round turret with a conical roof. There are eighty windows of various shapes set above limestone sills; they include round, oriel, semicircular, and oval as well as stained glass.

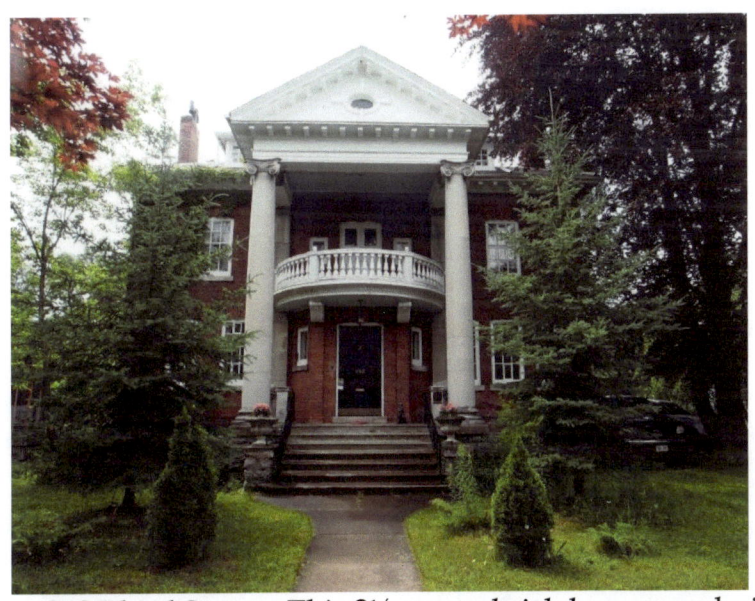

242 Third Street - This 2½ storey brick home was built for Charles Pitt, owner of the Bertram Lumber Company. John Wilson was the local Collingwood architect. The house was built in 1908 and is a Georgian influenced Neo-Classical home. A large pediment and column portico adorns the front façade. A balcony protrudes from the second floor within the pediment which has an elliptical window. Brick alternating radiating voussoirs adorn the window and door surround heads on the façade.

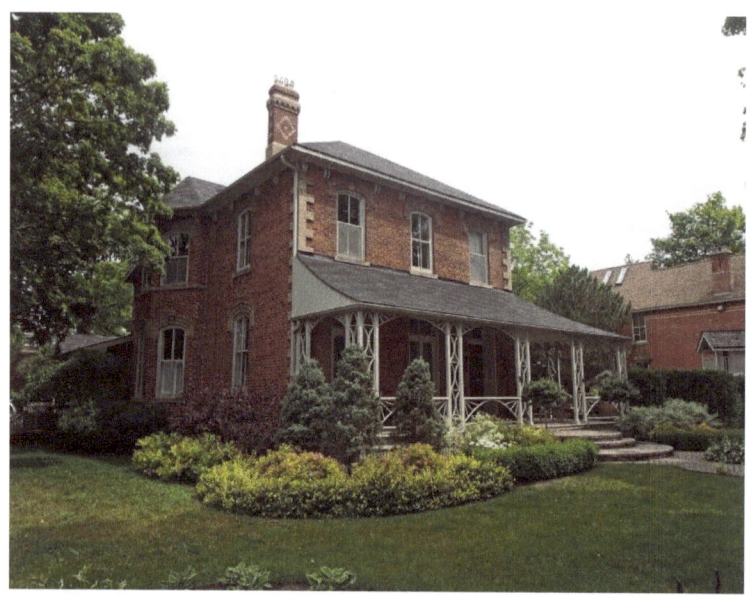

199 Third Street – Built in the Italianate tradition for the Toner family, early coal and lumber merchants, this home has retained its elegance with minor alterations since 1882. The interior of the home features a circular staircase, marble fireplaces, plaster medallions and a built in buffet.

The exterior brick work laid in the common bond tradition is highlighted by protruding quoins and plinth in lighter contrasting brick. Decorative brick work adorns the original chimney as well as highlighting the window openings. Brick arch work and keystones decorate the window surrounds in a unique three-tiered stepped arch design. The main front façade contains unique, French doors with recessed mullion and molded panels.

The home has a heavily bracketed low hip roof with an east side gable featuring a combination of corniced boxed brackets.

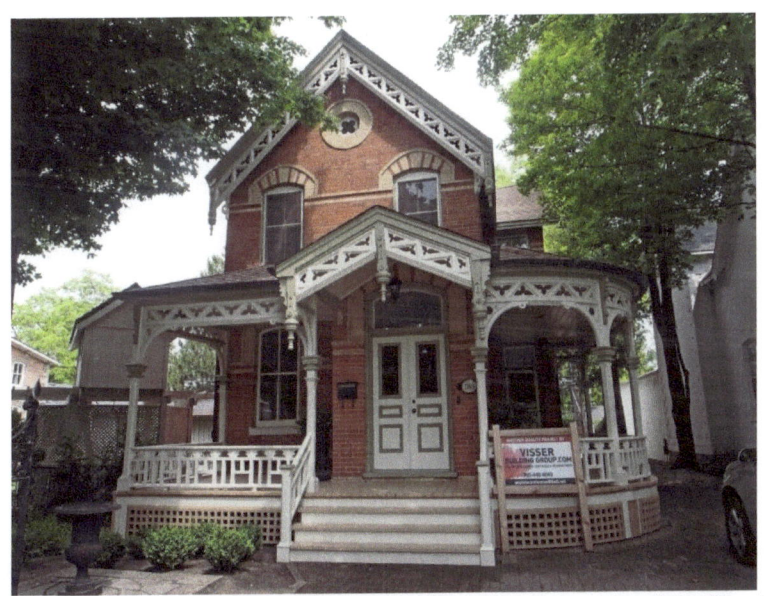

185 Third Street – elaborate verge board trim – Gothic Revival style – dichromatic brick work banding and window voussoirs

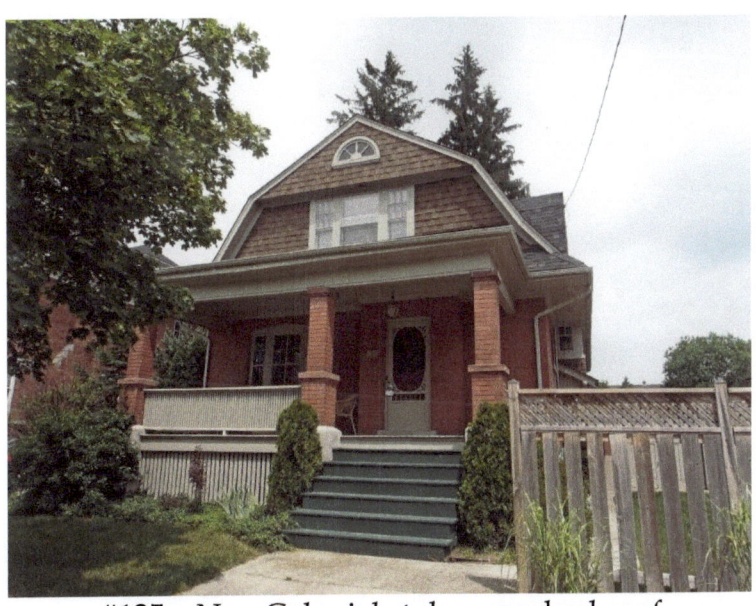

#125 – Neo-Colonial style – gambrel roof

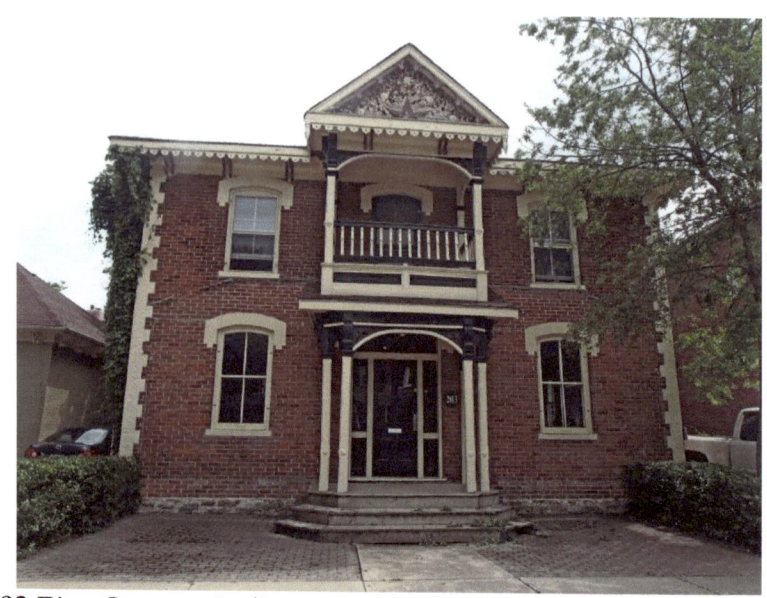

203 Pine Street – Italianate style – triangular pediment with decorated tympanum, lighter colored window hoods, double cornice brackets, frontispiece supported by pillars

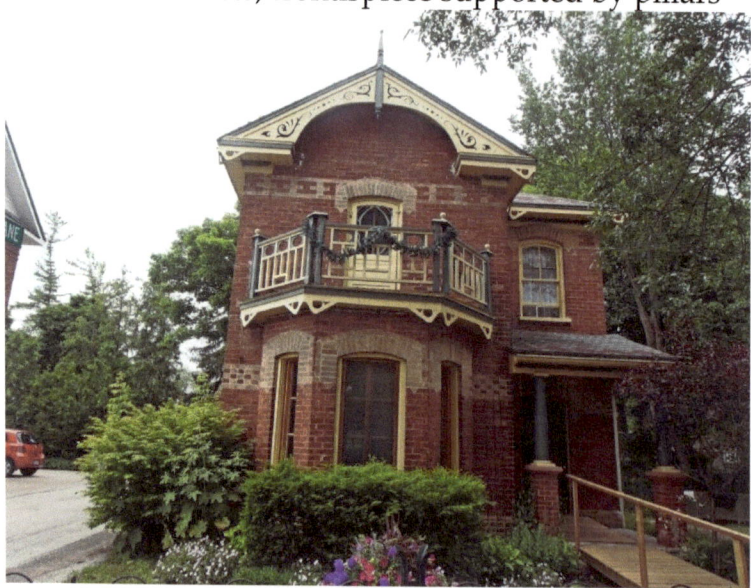

242 Pine Street - Italianate with Gothic style frontispiece, verge board and finial, dichromatic brickwork

Essex, Ontario – My Top 7 Picks

Amherstburg and Sandwich, the first towns to be established in Essex County, were first settled in 1796 after the British evacuated Fort Detroit. The populations of both towns were augmented by people emigrating from the United States to the south after the American Revolutionary War (1775-1783), especially from the City of Detroit by those who chose to remain British subjects, people known as "United Empire Loyalists".

After the American Revolution and the War of 1812 (1812-1815), people continued to migrate north to the area, and came from the east from Lake Ontario and the St. Lawrence River of Lower Canada seeking land. Settlers began to move eastward along the north shore of Lake Erie. Land was purchased from the Indians in the southern half of the current county. The British Court made land available for settlement provided that certain improvements were made to the land within a year and that it was not used for speculation. Settlers in the area included Hessians who fought for the British against the American rebels, and Pennsylvania Dutch (Mennonites).

In 1854 the Great Western Railway connected the Detroit frontier with the east, crossing Essex County. The Canadian terminal was in Windsor, which consequently forged ahead of the other towns of the county. Other railway lines were built that connected settlements in Kingsville, Harrow, Essex and Leamington.

By the late 19th century Essex County had seen fur trading and logging, land clearing and farming, road building and railway development, saw mills and gristmills, railway stations and water ports. By this time the forests were disappearing, replaced by fertile farmland.

Essex is a town in Essex County in southwestern Ontario with its municipal borders extending to Lake Erie. The Talbot Trail attributed to the growth of Essex in the last half of the 19th century.

Essex was one of the first counties to be settled in Upper Canada mostly by French people in the mid-18th century. Around 1749, the first permanent settlements began to appear on what is now the Canadian side of the Detroit River which despite its name is a strait connecting Lake Huron and the smaller Lake Saint Clair in the north and to Lake Erie in the south, as part of the Great Lakes system.

Essex County is largely composed of clay-based soils, with sandy soils along the beaches and shores. For the most part, Essex County is flat farmland, with some woodlots. When farmers first arrived, they encountered difficulty in trying to clear the extremely thick forests that covered Essex County. The farmers starved the trees from nourishment by cutting deep gashes in the bark, and burned them to clear the way to get to the fertile soils underneath. The fires were so intense that the reddish glow could be seen from Fort Chicago, 300 miles away, as millions of cords of wood burned.

On August 10, 1907, at the Essex Station there was a large explosion that sent shockwaves across the county and into some parts of nearby Michigan. A train cart containing 5000 pounds of nitroglycerine ignited. The blast sent debris over 600 yards away, killed two people and injured many more. The boom of the explosion caused plaster to fall from the ceilings of buildings in Windsor and windows to rattle as far as Detroit. The Essex Station was very heavily damaged. The Essex Station was rebuilt to its previous form and remains a recognizable landmark in the town.

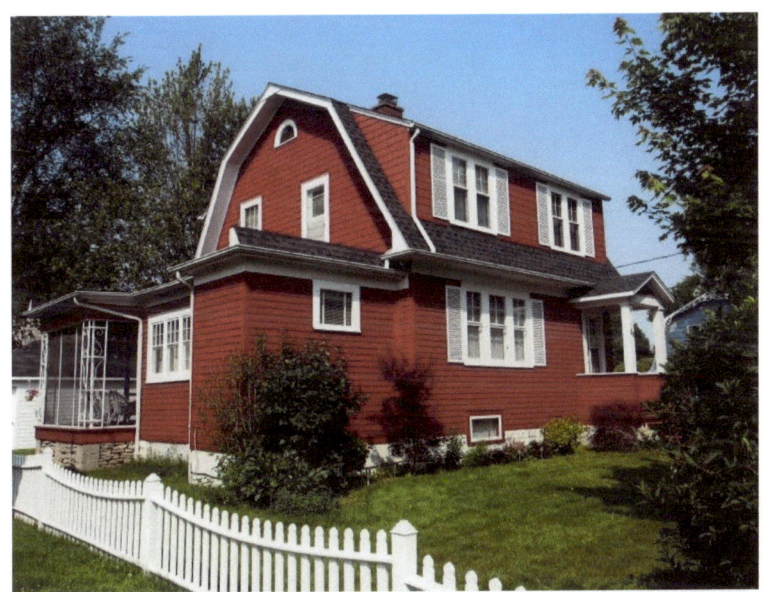

80 Irwin Avenue – Neo-Colonial style – gambrel roof

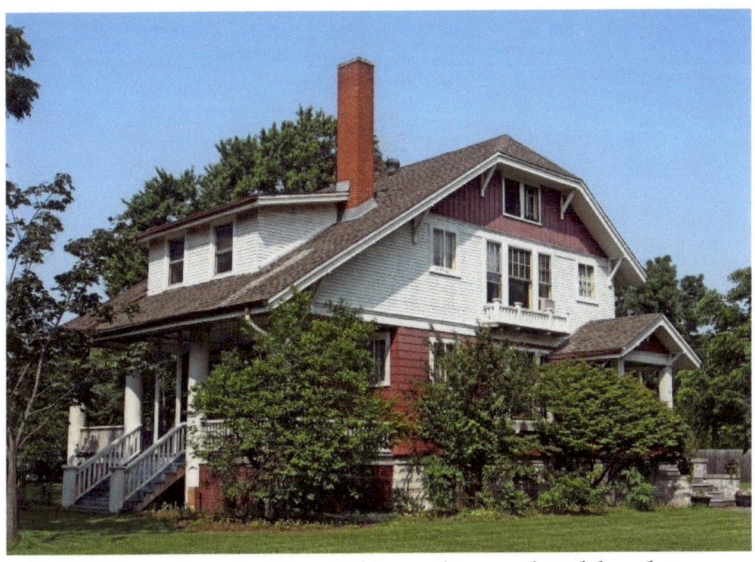

46 Alice Street – vernacular – chipped gable, dormer

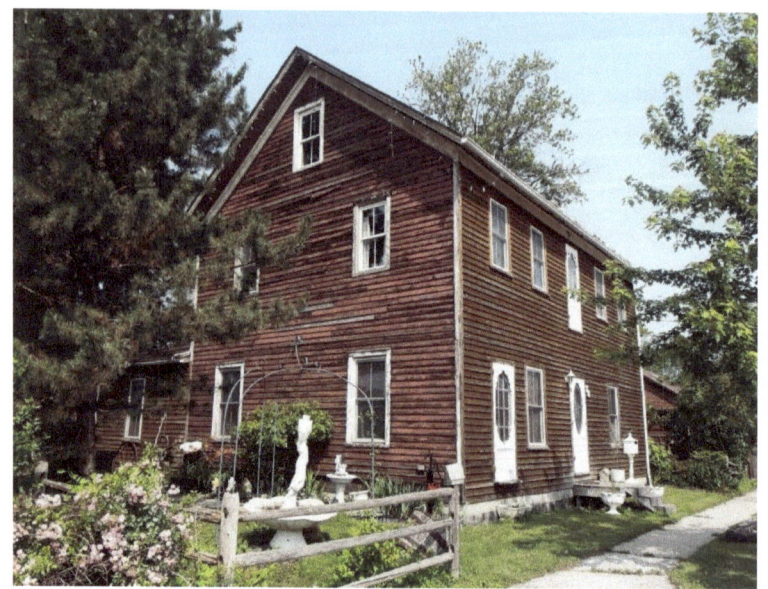
78 Fox Street – Gothic/Georgian style – wooden building

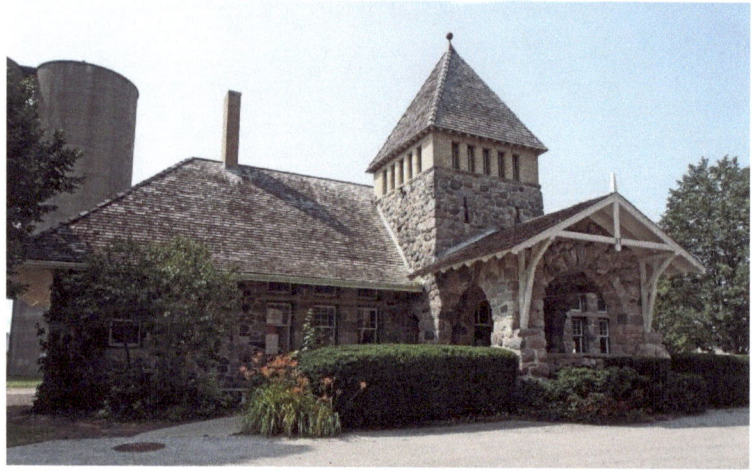
Essex Railway Station – stone train station – 1887

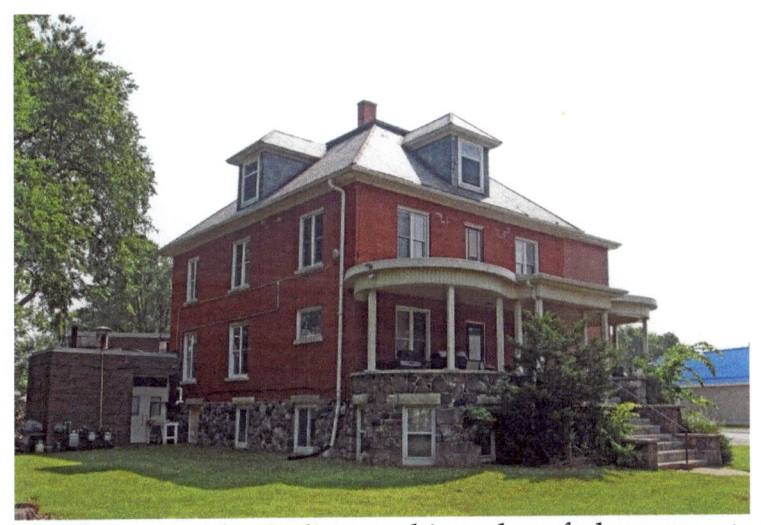

Talbot Street North – Italianate, hipped roof, dormers, stone basement walls

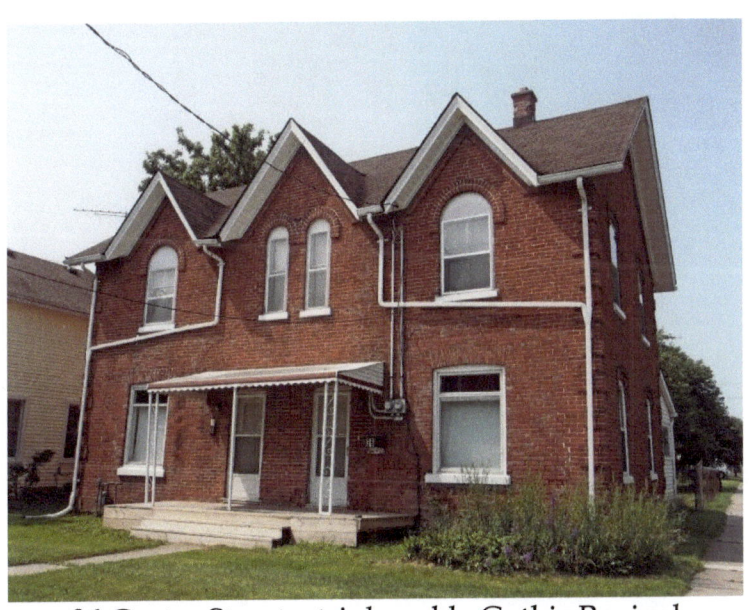

36 Centre Street – triple-gable Gothic Revival

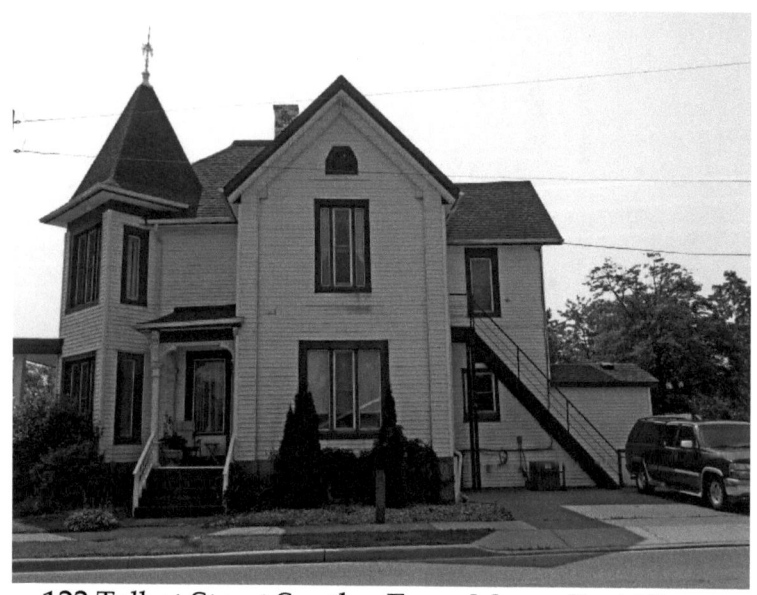

122 Talbot Street South – Essex Manor Rest Home
Two-storey, Queen Anne style

Kingsville, Ontario – My Top 12 Picks

Kingsville is located in Essex County in southwestern Ontario, west of Leamington, south of Lakeshore, southeast of Essex. It is primarily an agricultural community nestled along the north shore of Lake Erie. The terrain is generally flat, and consists of a mixture of various rocks, sand and clay. The town is about 570 feet above sea level.

Kingsville is home to the Jack Miner Bird Sanctuary. Jack Miner was awarded The Order of the British Empire (OBE) for his achievements in conservation in the British Empire. Jack Miner is considered "the father of the conservation movement on the continent".

The Town of Kingsville is rich in history and Victorian era architecture.

Kingsville bore witness first-hand to General Brock's historic journey to meet with Chief Tecumseh on August 13, 1812. This meeting led to the capture of Fort Detroit and British control of the Michigan frontier; more than 2,000 muskets were captured and used to arm Canadian militia units. In the later 1800s, Loyalists from the area fought in the Fenian raids; many served in World Wars I and II in an effort to preserve our history, our land, and our stake in the future.

Kingsville's harbour provides shelter for ships in need and provides commerce for the area.

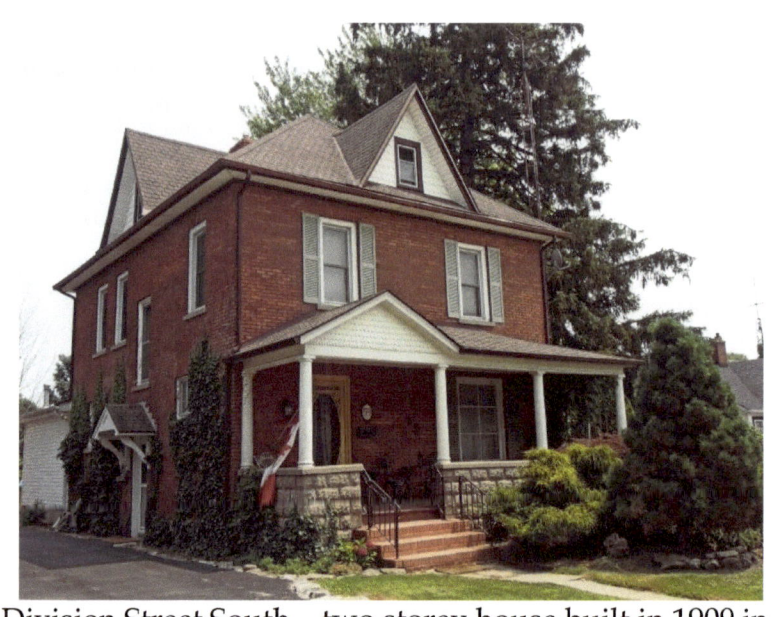

59 Division Street South – two storey house built in 1909 in the Colonial Revival style – cut fieldstone foundation, hip roof, Doric columns – Book 1

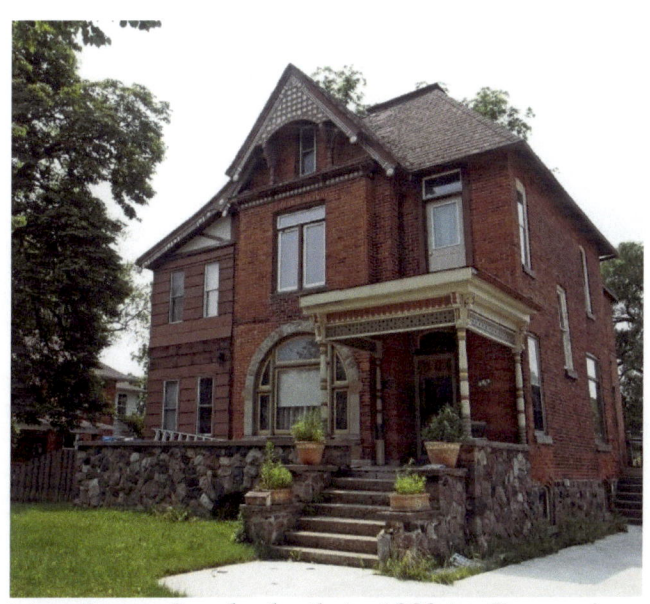

78 Division Street South– built in 1893 in Queen Anne style, front gable with basket weave cross-bracing with decorative verge boards, fretwork, 2½ storey rectangular bay with herringbone brick pattern to separate second storey from attic, cut fieldstone foundation, transom windows, large first storey arched window with rough and smooth stone surround – Book 1

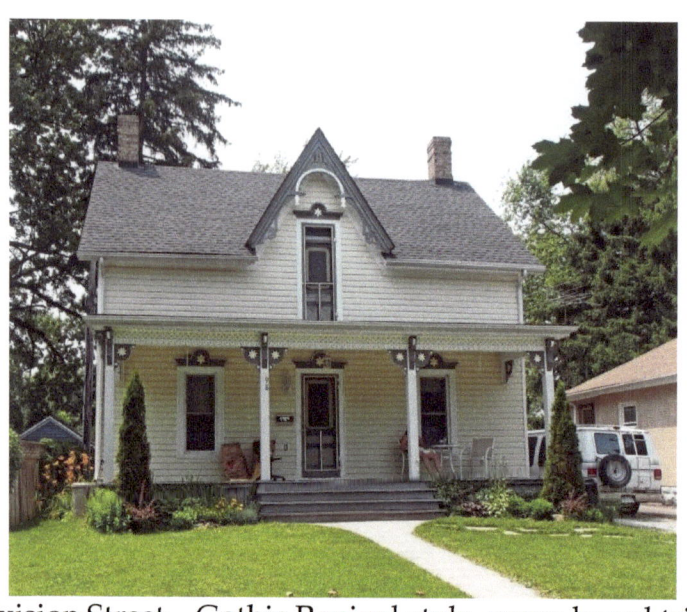

98 Division Street – Gothic Revival style, verge board trim on gable, decorative window hood above second floor door, decorative woodwork on verandah cornice and pillars
– Book 1

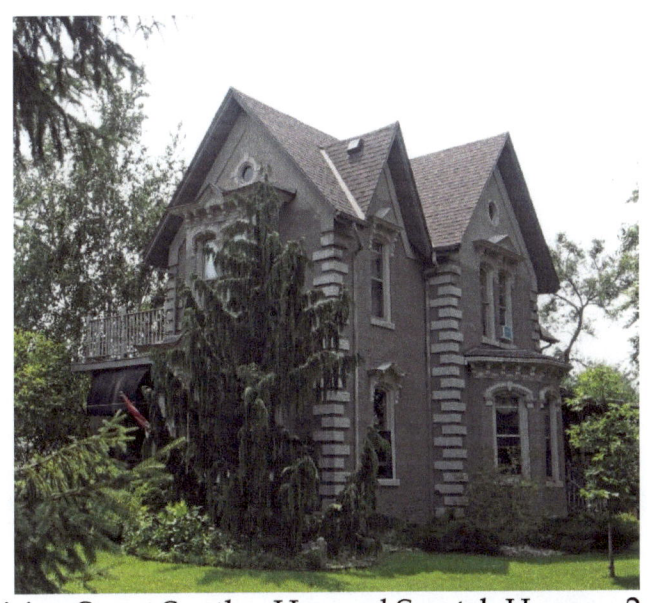

164 Division Street South – Howard Scratch House – 2 storey – 1886 – Italianate style (Scratch was a local tinsmith and bicycle factory owner) – asymmetrical design; brick quoins on corners; roundel windows in each of three large gables; 2-storey square bay on the front of the house; 1-storey angular bay on the north side; one-over-one double hung wood sash windows – Book 1

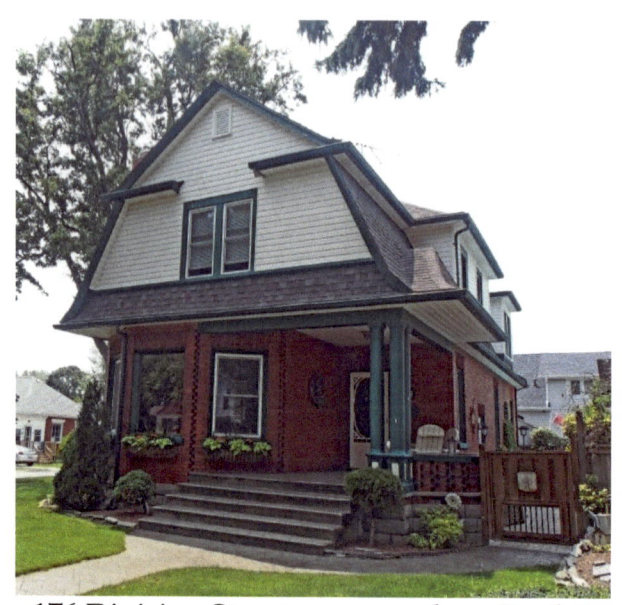

176 Division Street – vernacular – Book 1

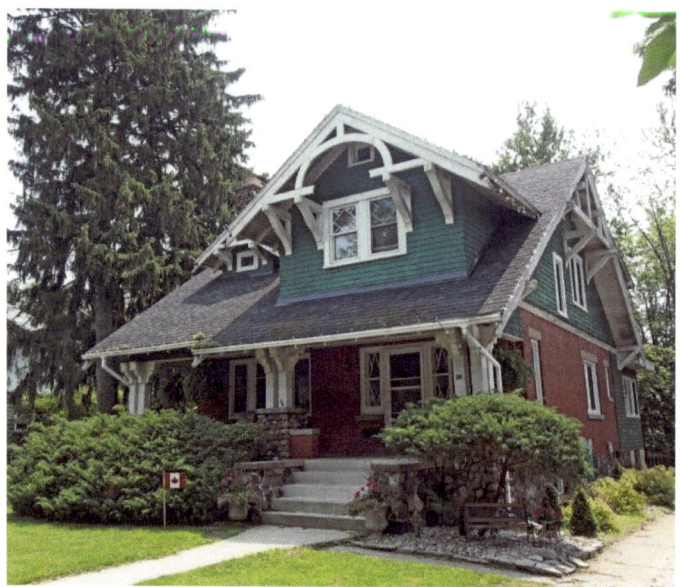

93 Main Street – vernacular – Book 1

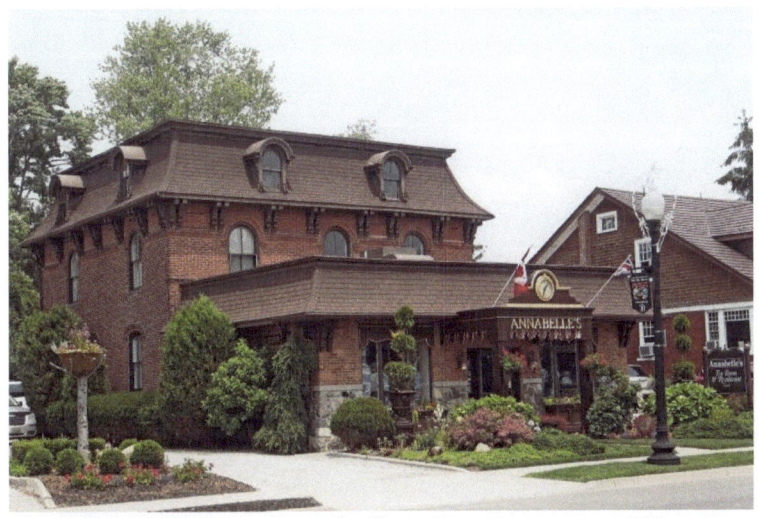

76 Main Street East – Annabelle's Tea House and Restaurant Built in 1859 – Second Empire style – dormers with window hoods in mansard roof, paired cornice brackets - Anna Belle Miriah Brien Evans was Susanne's grandmother, for whom tea was an essential part of her day. Tea time for her grandma was an institution. At 4 o'clock, as matter-of-factly as anything done on a regular basis, she would proceed to the kitchen as if reminded by an internal clock. Susanne would get the small china tea set and set the table by the window in the dining room. There, as the sunlight streamed in, they would sip tea, have a biscuit, or two, and talk about the day. – Book 1

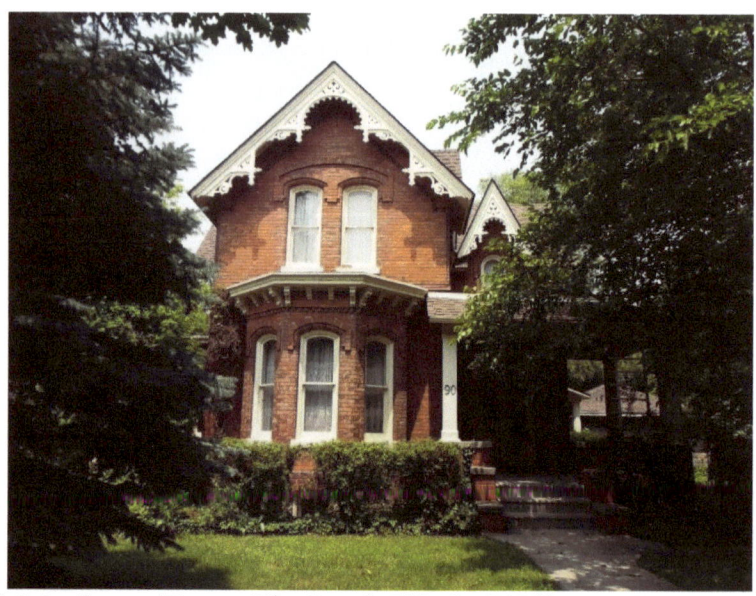

90 Main Street East – The Jacob Wigle/William Mortan Webb House built 1886 – Gothic Revival – verge board trim on gable, bay window, decorative brickwork including sawtooth designs, hood moulds over the windows – Book 1

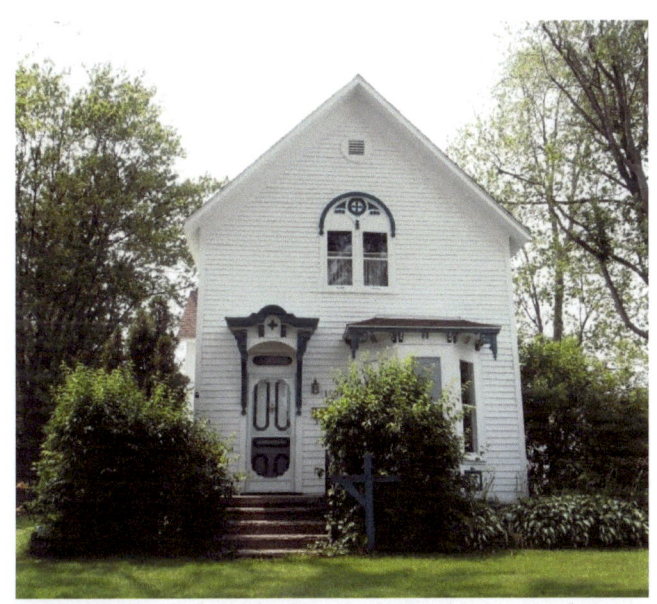

160 Queen Street – hood above door, bay window, cornice brackets – Book 2

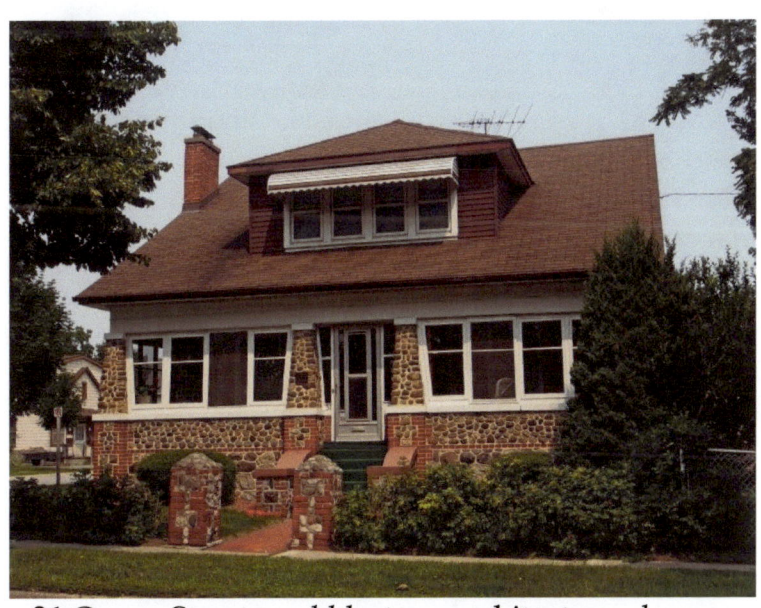

31 Queen Street – cobblestone architecture, dormer Arts and Crafts style – Book 2

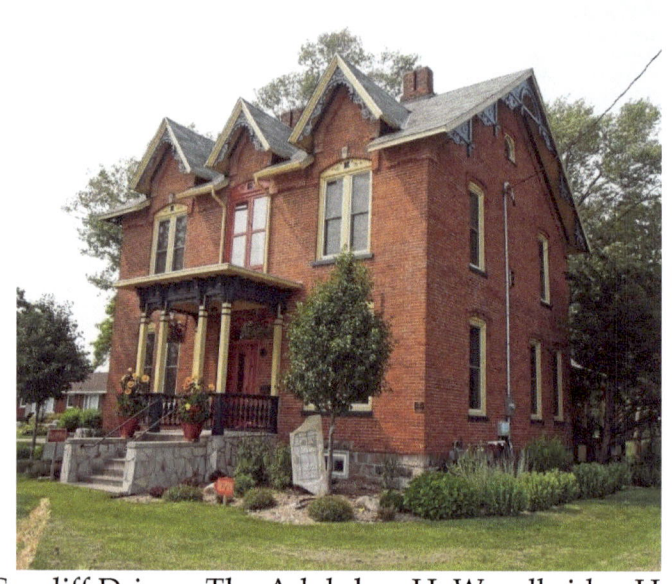

608 Seacliff Drive – The Adolphus H. Woodbridge House - Bed and Breakfast – built 1881 – triple gable Gothic Revival, verge board trim on gables with stenciling, cornice brackets on porch, window voussoirs with keystones, stenciling above windows; cut fieldstone foundation – Book 2

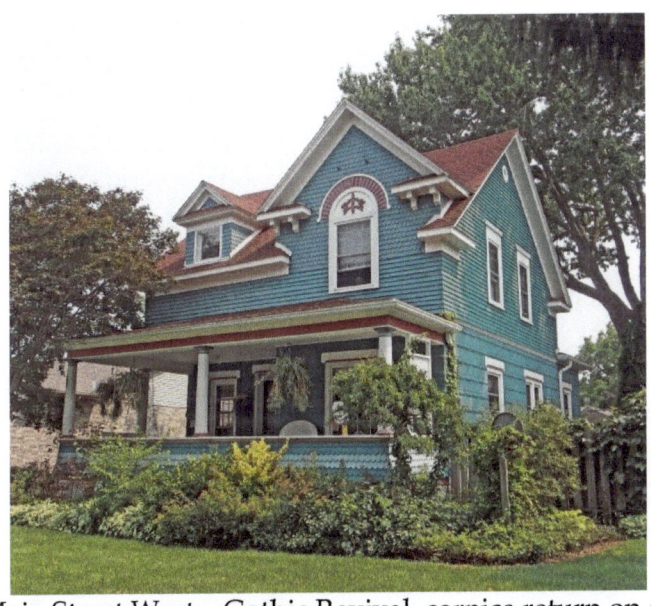

119 Main Street West – Gothic Revival, cornice return on gables with cornice brackets, dormer, fishscale patterning in gable and dormer, doric pillars for verandah supports – Book 2

Woodstock, Ontario – My Top 16 Picks

Woodstock is located in the heart of South Western Ontario, at the junction of highways 401 and 403, 50 km east of London and 60 km west of Kitchener. Woodstock is the largest municipality in Oxford County, a county known for its rich farmland, and for its dairy and cash crop farming. As well as being "The Dairy Capital of Canada", Woodstock also has a large industrial base, much of which is related to the auto manufacturing industry.

In 1792, Sir John Graves Simcoe became Lieutenant Governor of Upper Canada and made plans for the development of the interior of Upper Canada. He envisioned a series of town sites linked by a military road and a system of rivers and canals, providing inland access during an era when commerce and settlements depended on major waterways. London, Chatham, Dorchester and Oxford were designated town sites with London as the defensible capital. The military road stretching from Burlington Bay through Woodstock to London provided an overland supply route for the safe movement of troops and settlers. Simcoe named this road Dundas Street after Henry Dundas, Viscount Melville, Secretary of State for War and the Colonies.

To speed development in the sparsely populated interior of the province, Simcoe granted whole townships to land companies who were obligated to bring in settlers.

Simcoe passed through the area now known as Woodstock and noted it a suitable "Town Plot" and settlement began here in 1800.

In the 1830s, a different group of immigrants were encouraged to settle in Oxford to ensure this community's loyalty to the British crown. British naval and army officers placed on half-pay looked to the colonies for a new career at the conclusion of military service. The first to arrive was Alexander Whalley Light, a retired colonel who came to Oxford County in 1831. He was joined by Philip Graham in 1832, a retired captain of the Royal Navy, and Captain Andrew Drew, on half-pay from the Royal Navy, arrived in Woodstock to make preparations for his superior, Rear-Admiral Henry Vansittart, also on half-pay. Half-pay officers went to considerable lengths to clear their chosen parcels of land.

Admiral Vansittart commissioned Colonel Andrew Drew to build a church (Old St. Paul's) in a new area of Oxford that was known as the "Town Plot". The men later quarreled, which led to the construction of a second church known as "New St. Paul's".

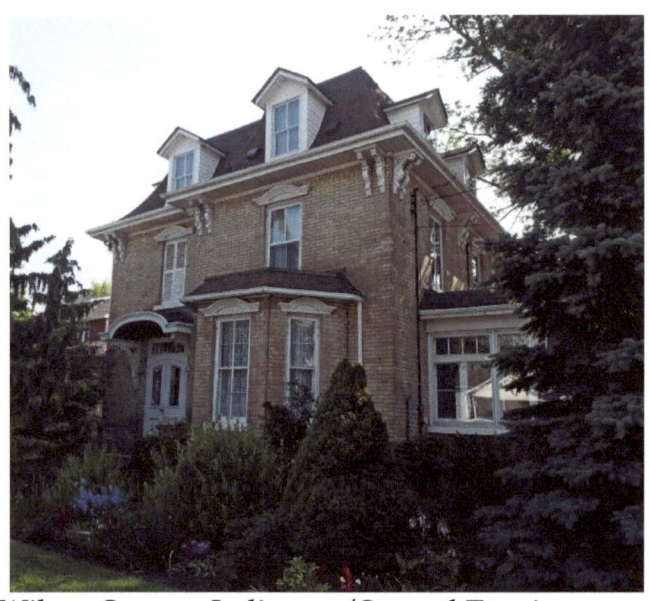

73 Wilson Street – Italianate/Second Empire – type of mansard roof with dormers, paired cornice brackets, bay window, window hoods – Book 1

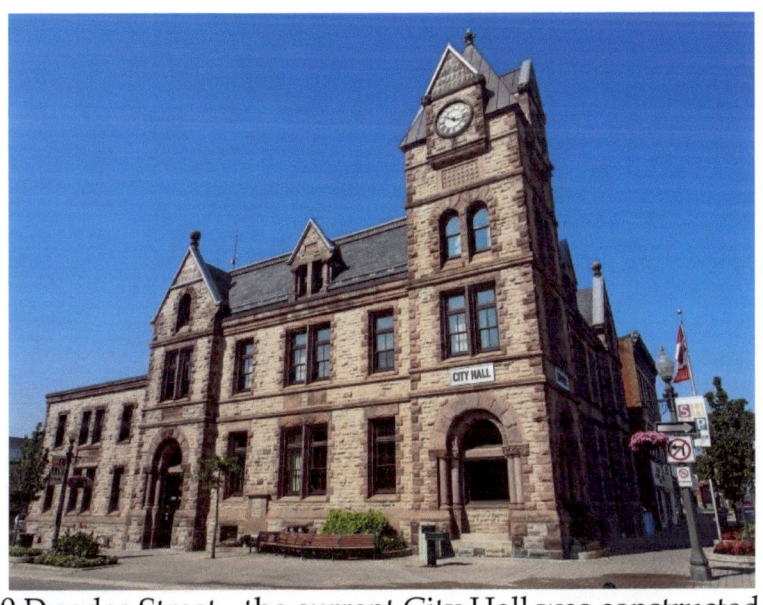

500 Dundas Street - the current City Hall was constructed of warm sandstone in 1899 as a post office; for over one hundred years it has been the centre of the municipal and social life of Woodstock. The corner tower has four clocks. It housed the local government and served as lecture hall, opera house, and assize court. It is basically eighteenth century Palladian architecture. Round- headed windows with heavy surrounds reflect Italianate Revival – Book 1

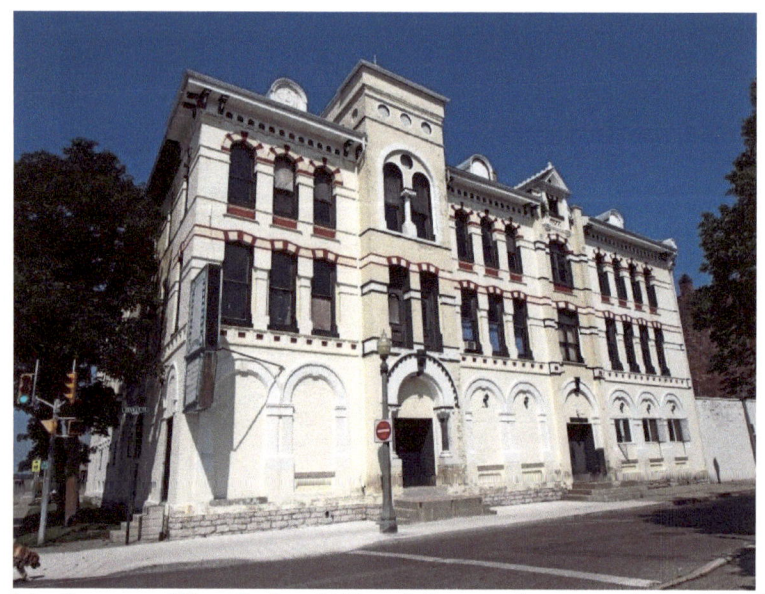

Finkle Street – The Oxford Hotel, located across from Market Square and the Town Hall in Woodstock was built in 1880 as "The O'Neill House" in Romanesque style. It saw guests such as Oscar Wilde and Reginald Birchall. – Book 1

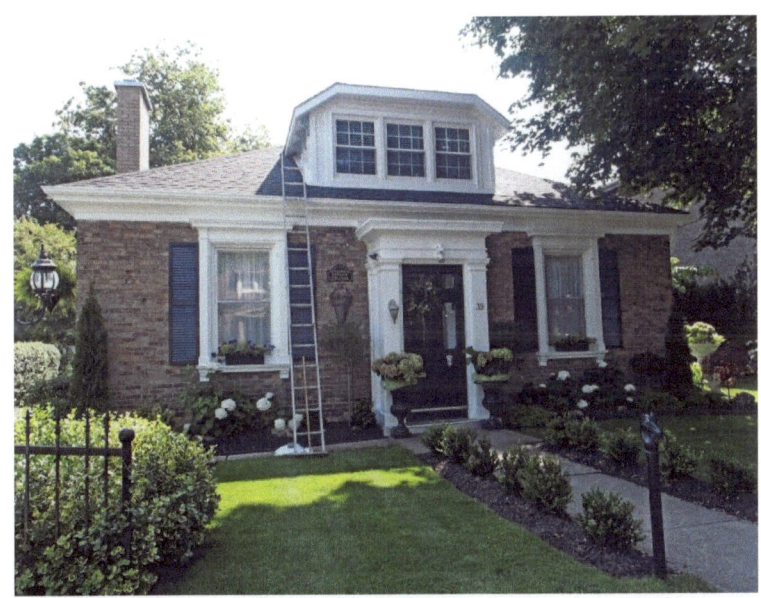

39 Victoria Street – Neo-Classical cottage is a 1½ storey buff brick home, hip roof, centred dormer; windows have wooden lintels and brackets supporting the sills; three panel double door on the storm porch has an interesting window shape in the door; field stone foundation – Book 1

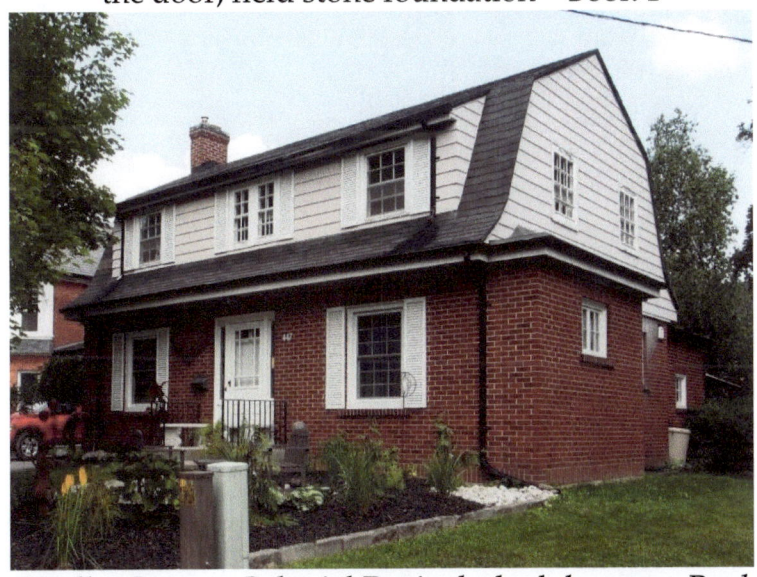

447 Buller Street – Colonial Revival, shed dormer – Book 1

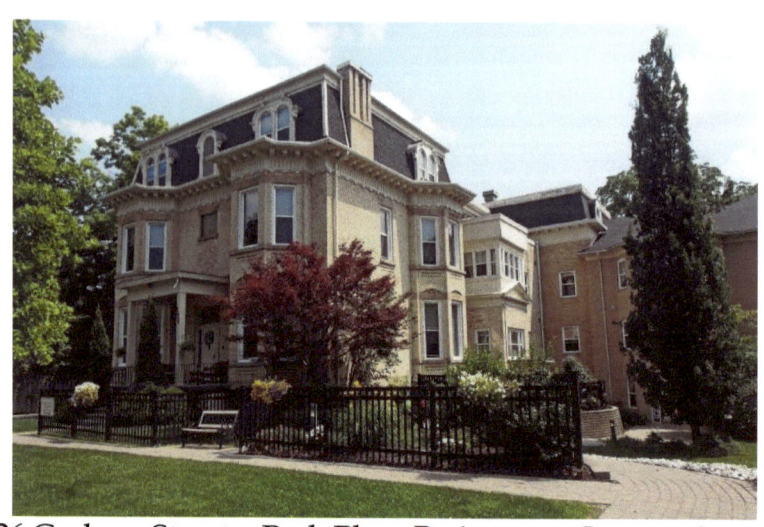

126 Graham Street – Park Place Retirement Centre - Second Empire style – mansard roof, window hoods, decorative cornice – Book 1

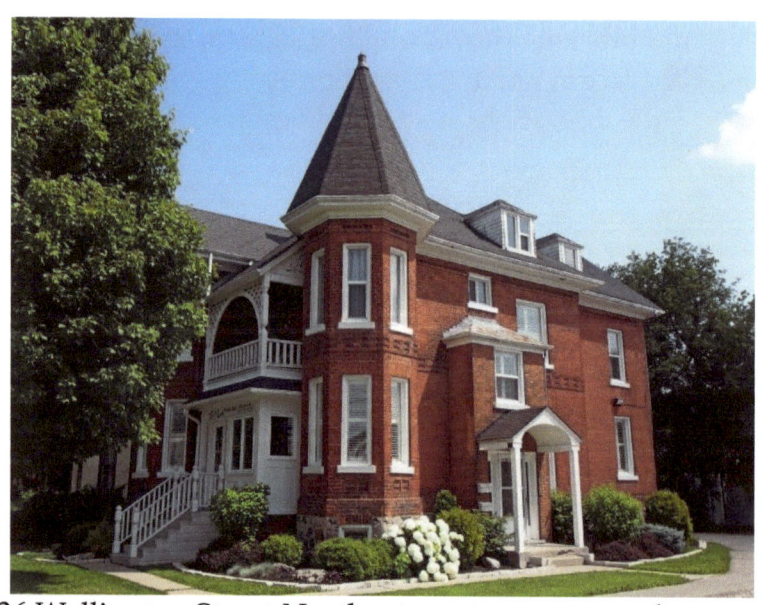

36 Wellington Street North – two storey turret, dormers, second floor balcony with spindle decorative work – Book 2

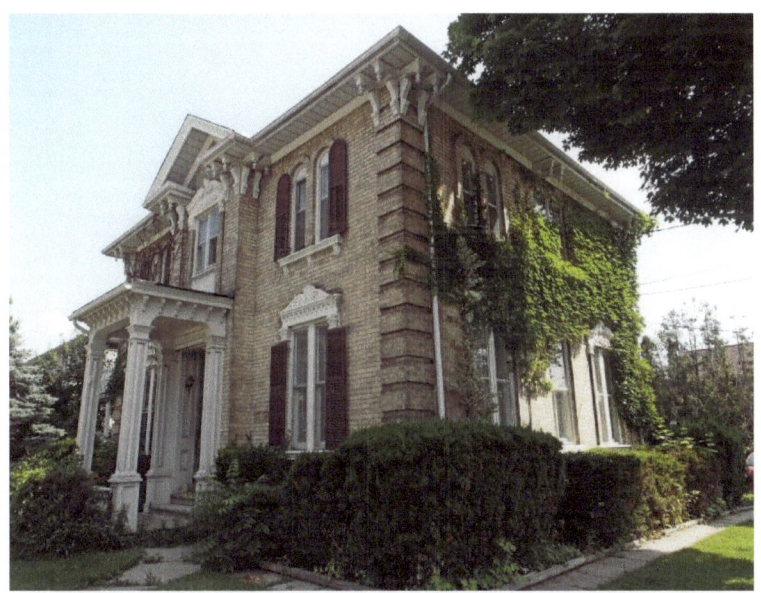

48 Wellington Street – Italianate, hipped roof, paired cornice brackets, window hoods, corner quoining, entrance – Book 2

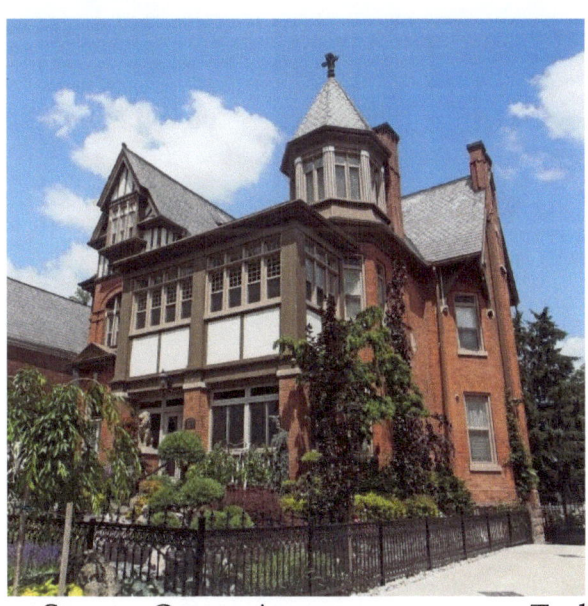

419 Drew Street – Queen Anne – turret, some Tudor style detailing – Book 2

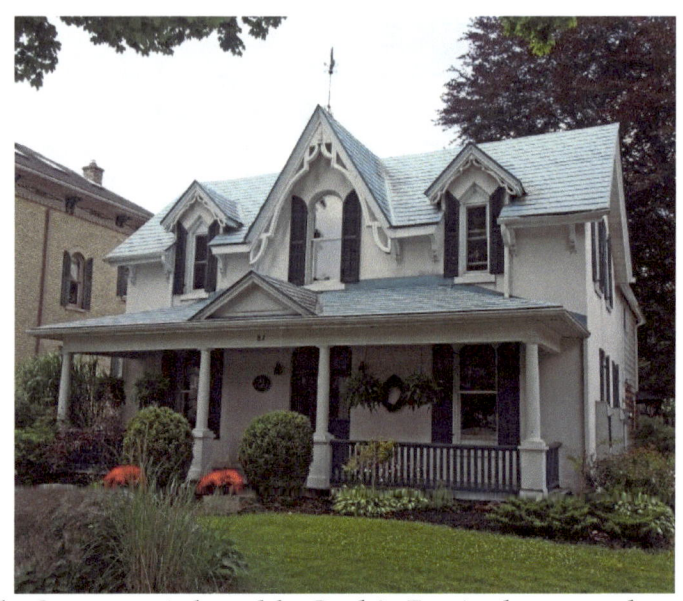

81 Light Street – triple gable Gothic Revival – verge board trim on gables, pediment – Book 2

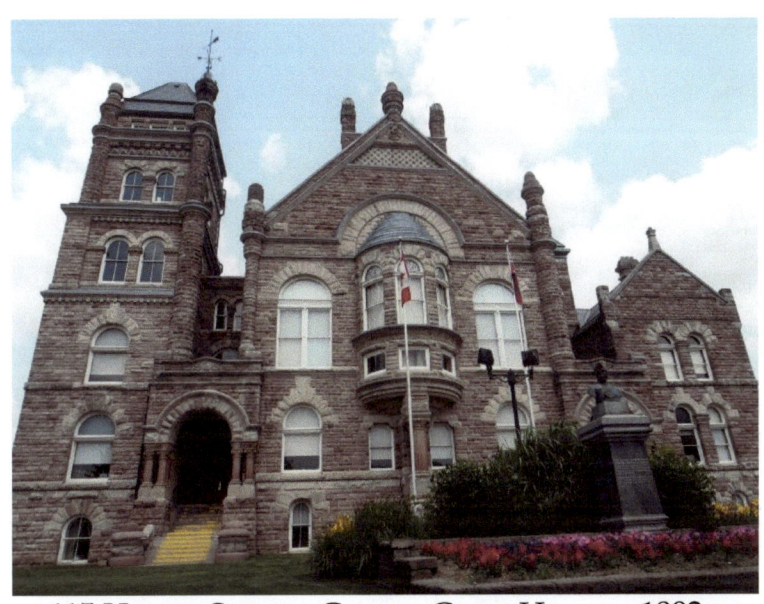

415 Hunter Street – County Court House – 1892 – a massive building of sandstone in the Richardsonian Romanesque style, with a complex roof line; oriel window; monkey heads are hidden among the capitals of the red marble pillars at the two front entrances, and there is a monkey at the peak – Book 3

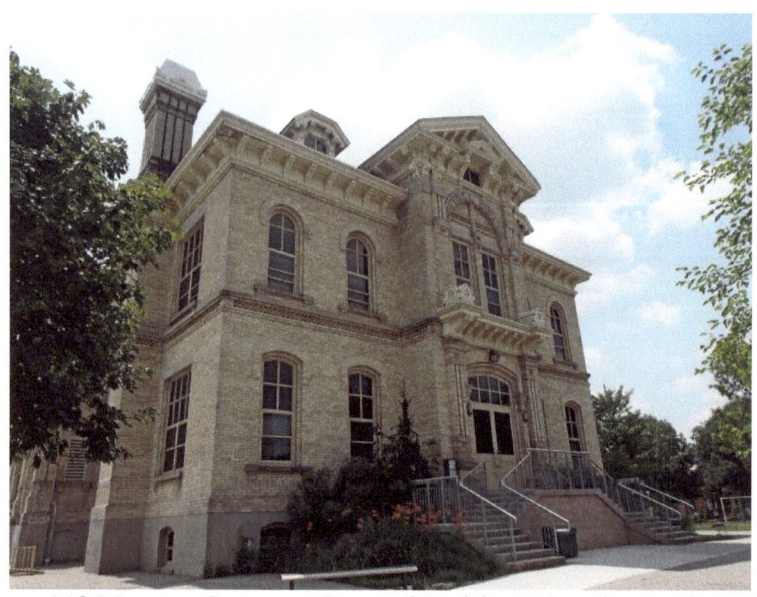

410 Hunter Street – Central Public School – built in 1880 – two impressive identical entrances, decorative brickwork separating the first and second floors, decorative gables on a steeply pitched roof, cornice brackets, saw tooth dentiling – Book 3

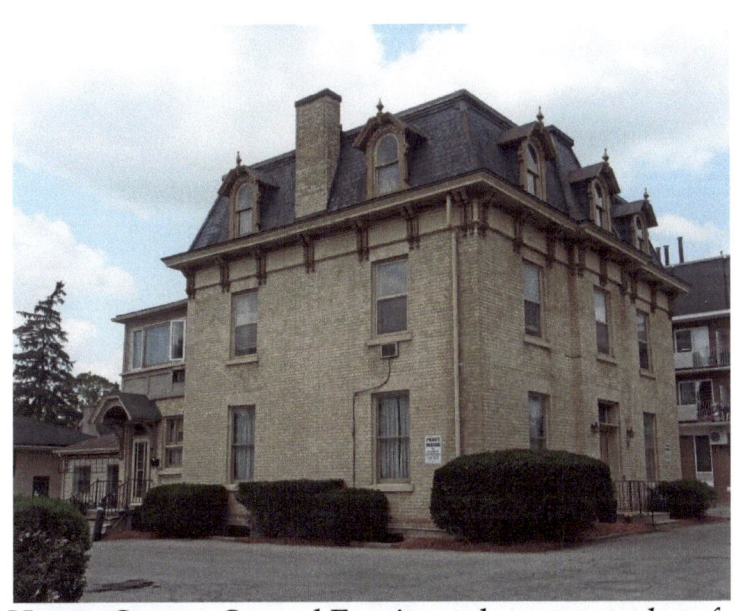

393 Hunter Street – Second Empire style – mansard roof with dormers with finials on window hoods, cornice brackets – Book 3

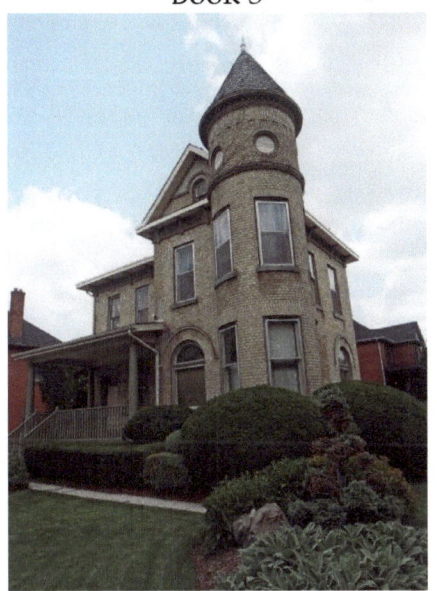

369 Hunter Street – Queen Anne – 2½ storey turret, Romanesque style window voussoirs, cornice brackets – Book 3

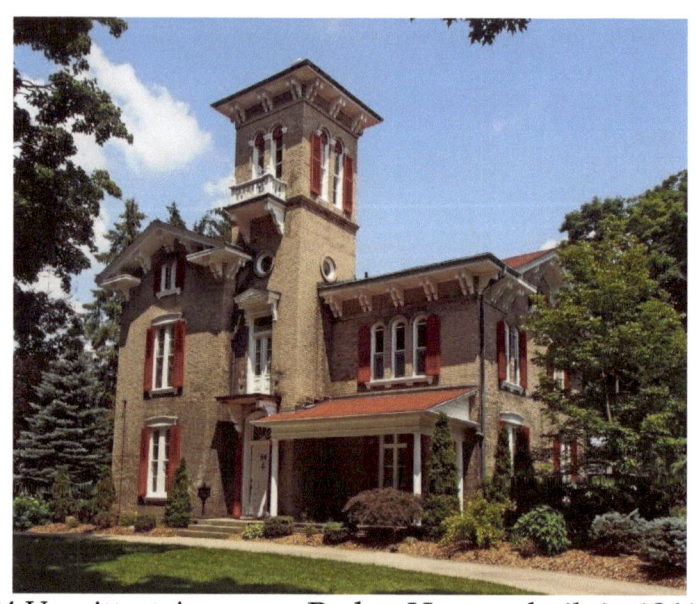

84 Vansittart Avenue – Parker House – built in 1864 - Italianate villa, small balconies, round-headed windows in groups, paired ornamental brackets supporting the roof, 3½ storey tower with decorative finial – Book 3

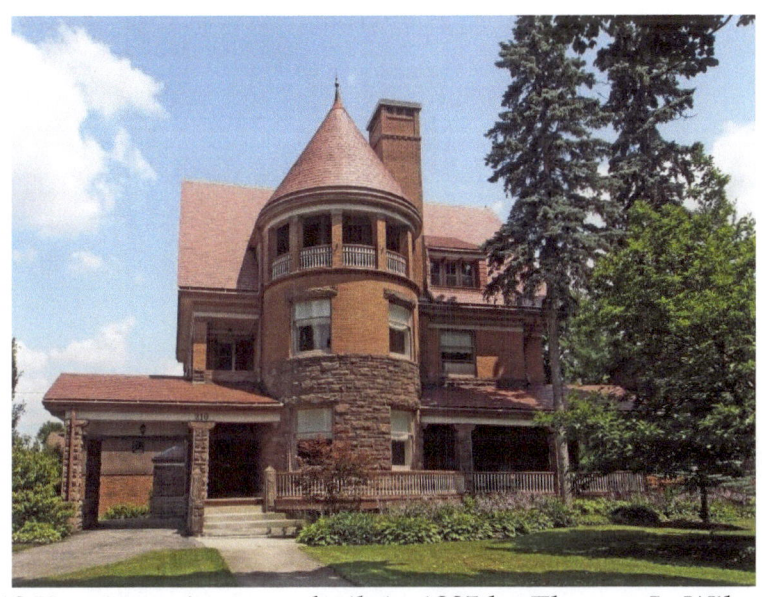

210 Vansittart Avenue - built in 1895 by Thomas L. Wilson, inventor of the first commercial calcium-carbide process for the manufacturer of acetylene gas. It was the residence of the Sisters of St. Joseph's until 1975. It is a voluptuous house of irregular shape in Richardsonian Romanesque style using contrasting brick, cut stone and hanging tiles; offset tower with balcony and verandah, portico at the front entrance – Book 3

Thamesford, Ontario – My Top 8 Picks

Oxford County is located in the heart of Southwestern Ontario and is made up of eight lower tier Municipalities. Zorra Township is located at the north-west corner of Oxford County. It is a rural municipality, and was formed in 1975 through the amalgamation of East Nissouri, West Zorra and North Oxford townships. The township includes the communities of Banner, Bennington, Brooksdale, Brown's Corners, Cody's Corners, Dicksons Corners, Dunn's Corner, Embro, Golspie, Granthurst, Harrington, Harrington West, Holiday, **Kintore**, Lakeside, Maplewood, McConkey, **Medina**, Rayside, **Thamesford, Uniondale**, Youngsville, and Zorra Station.

Kintore, Medina, Thamesford and Uniondale are included in this book of photos.

Thamesford is located on the western boundary of Oxford County, half way between London and Woodstock on Highway 2 (County Road 68) and between St. Mary's and Ingersoll on Highway 19.

Thames Centre is a municipality in Middlesex County east of the City of London. It was formed on January 1, 2001, when the townships of West Nissouri and North Dorchester were amalgamated. Communities in the township include: Avon, Belton, Cherry Grove, Crampton, Cobble Hill, Derwent, Devizes, Dorchester, Evelyn, Fanshawe Lake, Friendly Corners, Gladstone, Harrietsville, Kelly Station, Mossley, Nilestown, Oliver, **Putnam**, Salmonville, Silvermoon, Thorndale, Three Bridges, and Wellburn. Putnam is included in this book of photos.

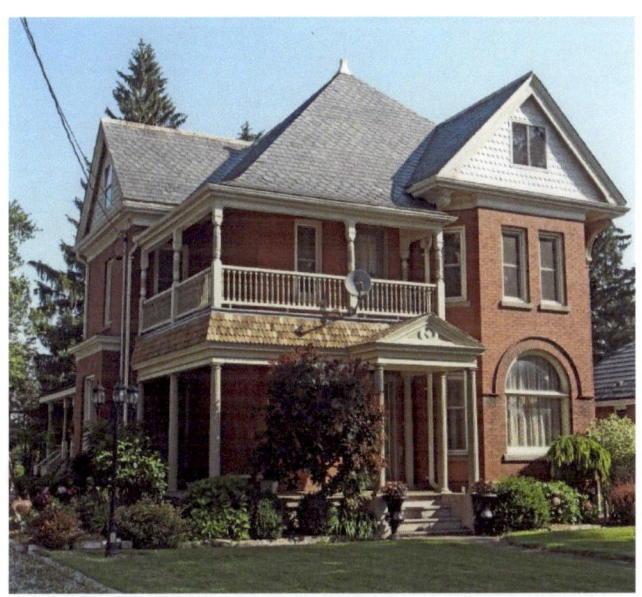

128 Delatre Street West – St. Andrew's Manse 1897 - "sleeping porch" on second floor, turned wood spindle supports, fretwork, pediment with decorated tympanum

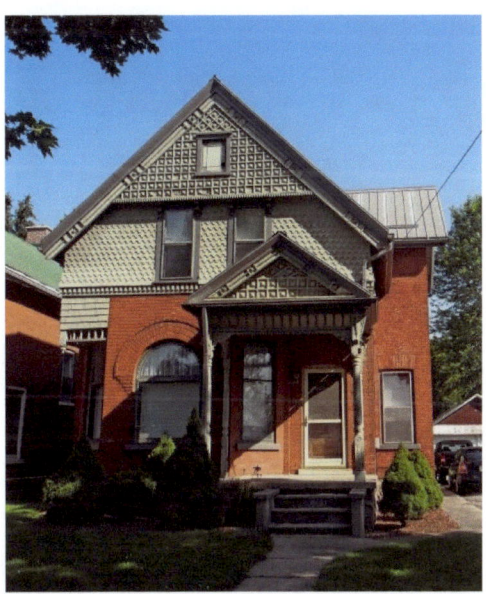

118 Delatre Street West – decorative gable and pediment, Romanesque style window voussoirs

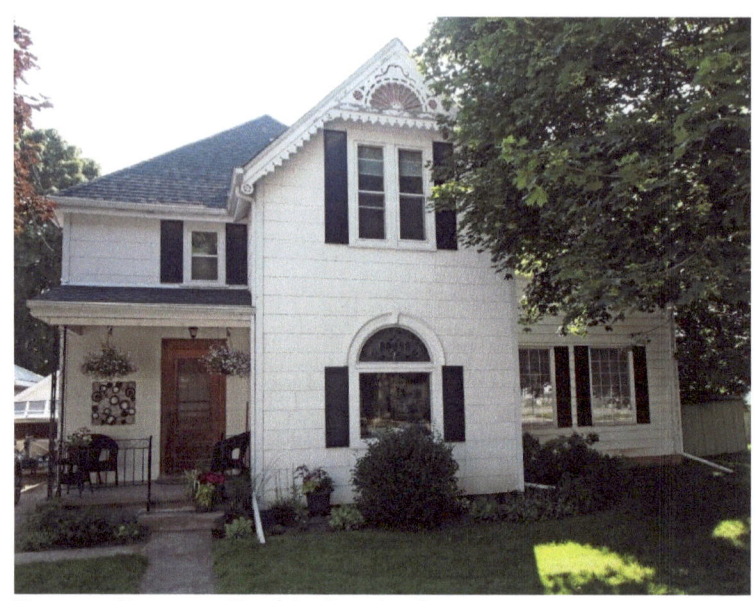

George Street – Gothic Revival - within peak of gable is a decorative arch with applied scrollwork, spindles and circular piercing

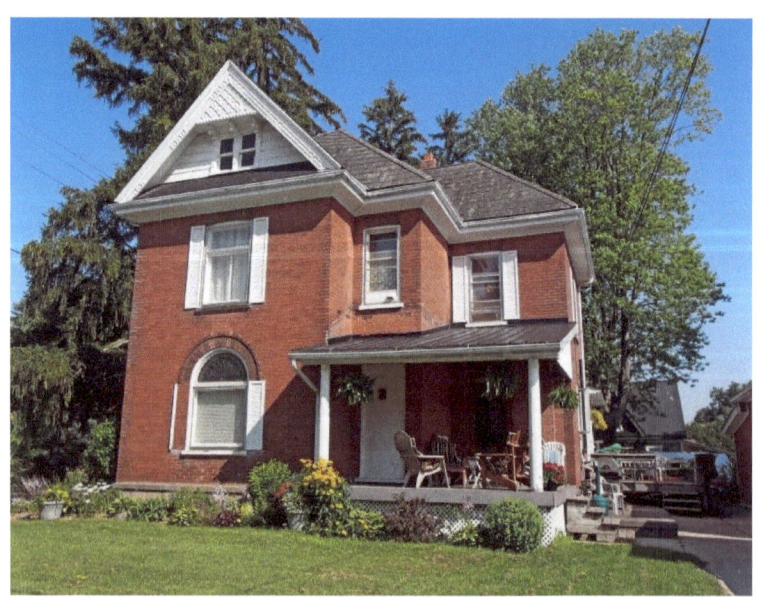

Washington Street – Edwardian, decorative gable

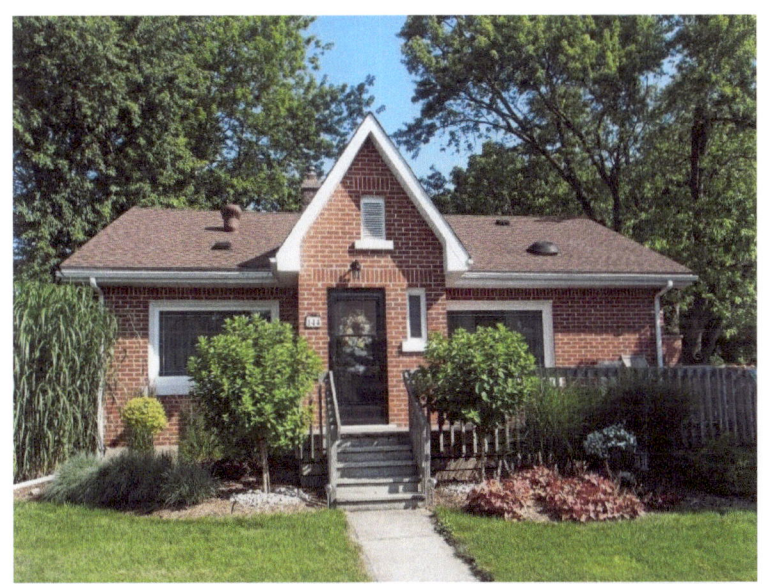

144 Washington Street – Regency cottage

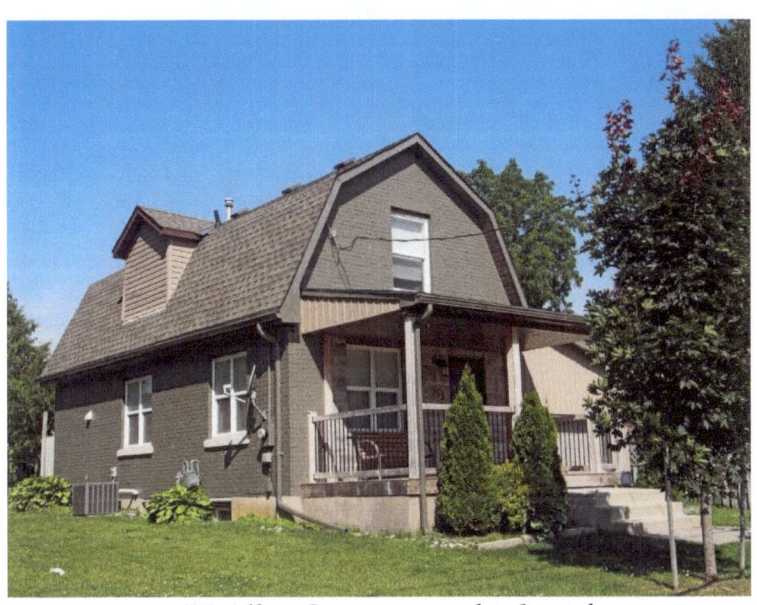

155 Allen Street – gambrel roof

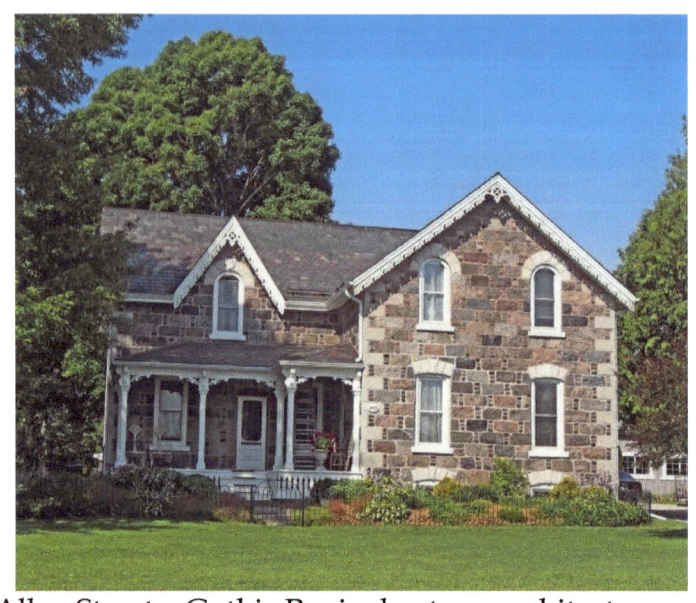

205 Allen Street – Gothic Revival - stone architecture, corner quoins

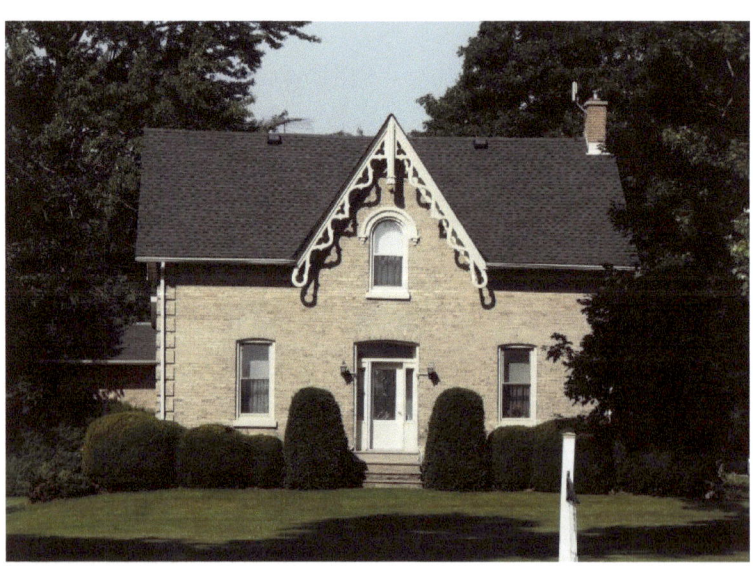

Gothic Revival, verge board trim on gable with finial

St. Marys, Ontario – My Top 13 Picks

St. Marys is a town in southwestern Ontario located southwest of Stratford. The north branch of the Thames River flows through St. Marys and is the heart of the town. St. Marys' early economic success depended on the mills, powered by the water in this river. The town's prosperity was also helped by the presence of accessible limestone, taken in blocks from the riverbed and from quarries along the riverbanks. The name "Stonetown" is an apt moniker for St. Marys, as the town is filled with unique architecture featuring locally-quarried limestone. The stone buildings reveal much about the town's history, and the development of the town can be witnessed in the architecture.

John Grieve Lind (1867-1947) was closely associated with the start of the St. Mary's Cement Company. St. Marys was chosen as the location for the plant because of its abundance of limestone, clay and water, it was on two national railway lines, and it had access to hydro-electric power from Niagara Falls. The plant opened in 1912. Once the cement plant was in operation, Lind turned his attention to parks and recreation. He purchased the seven acre Cadzow Park on Church Street South and build Cadzow Pool. Lind Park has a statue of Arthur Meighen, Canada's ninth prime minister.

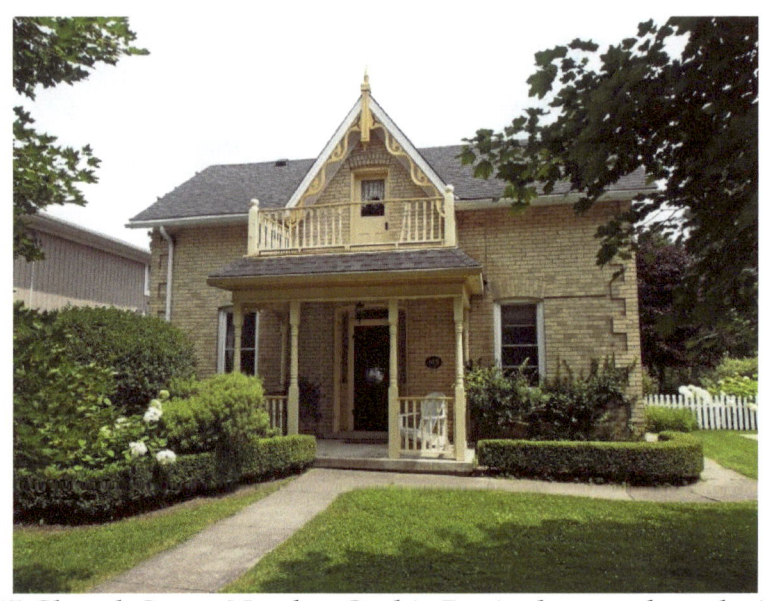

145 Church Street North – Gothic Revival, verge board trim and finial on gable, corner quoins, wood turned porch supports, sidelights and transom window surrounding door – St Marys Book 1

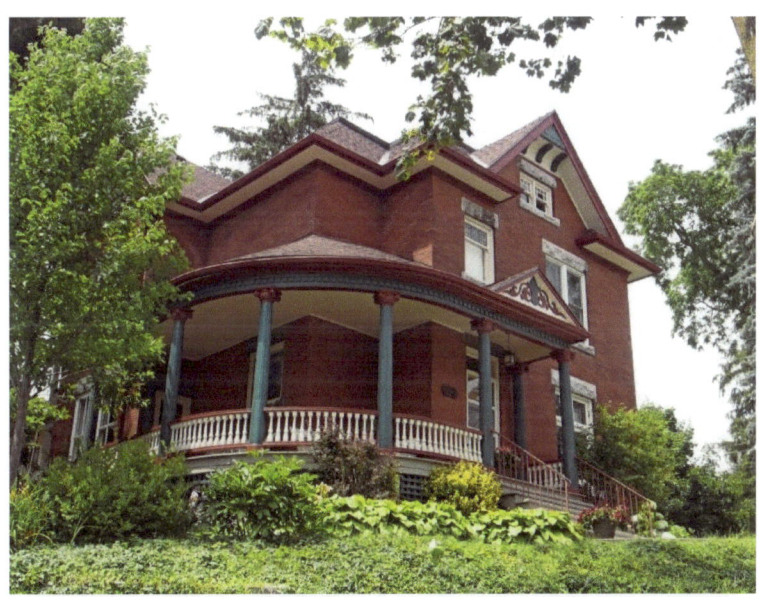

112 Church Street North – pediment with decorated tympanum, wraparound veranda

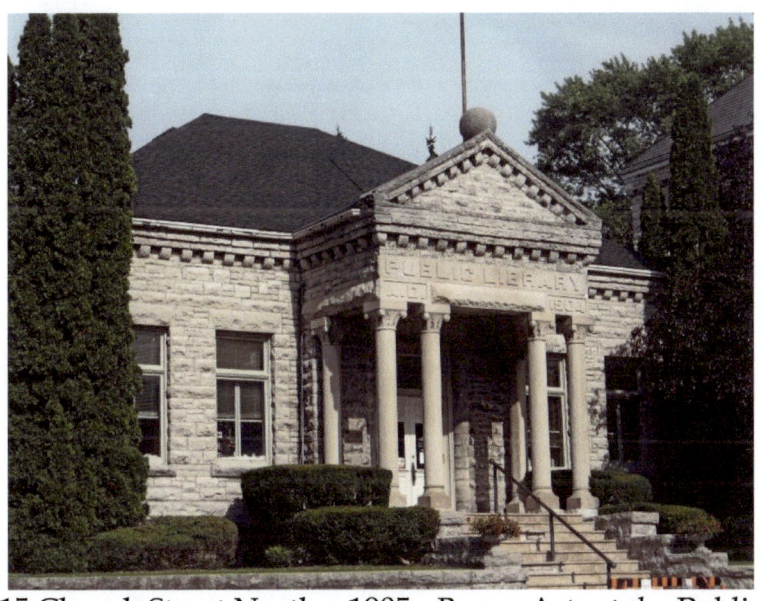

15 Church Street North – 1905 - Beaux Arts style, Public Library built of St. Marys limestone – pediment with dentil molding, pillars with Corinthian capitals

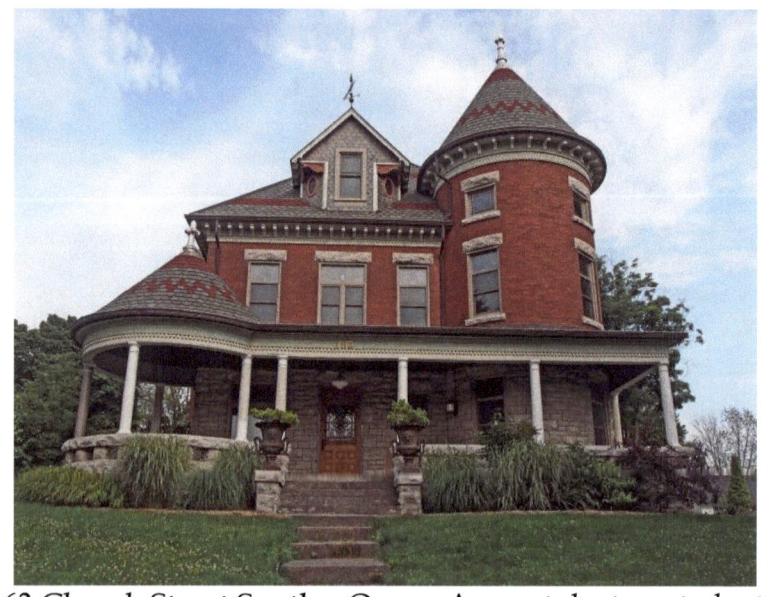

163 Church Street South – Queen Anne style, turret, dentil moulding, dichromatic tile work, wraparound verandah

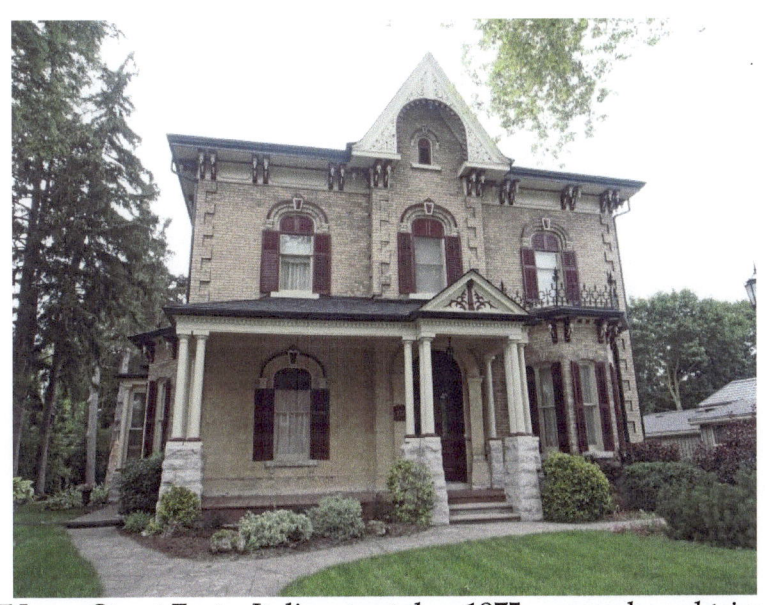

217 Jones Street East – Italianate style – 1875 – verge board trim on gable, cornice brackets, pediment with decorated tympanum, pillars with Doric capitals supporting verandah, bay window with iron cresting above, corner quoins, curved window voussoirs with keystones

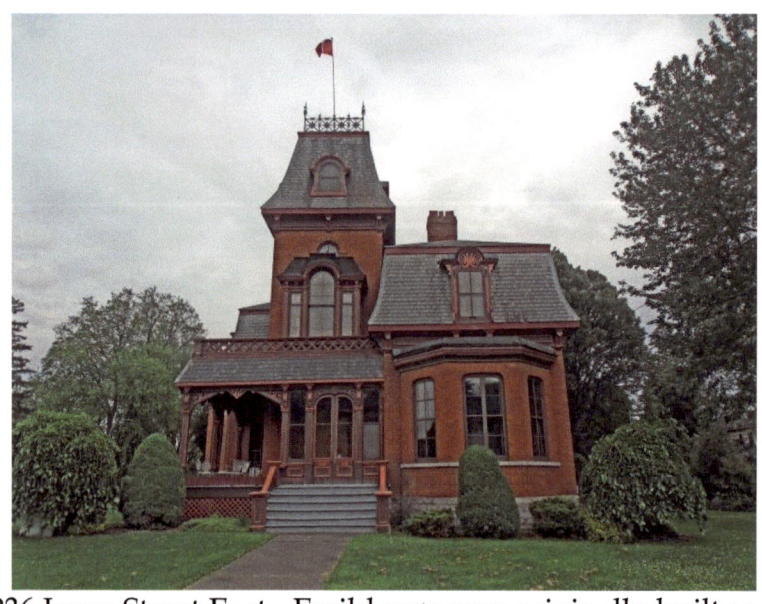

236 Jones Street East - Ercildoune was originally built as a wedding gift to George Carter's daughter Charlotte when she married Henry Lincoln Rice in 1880. The home is built in the Second Empire style, a very rare style of home in St. Marys.

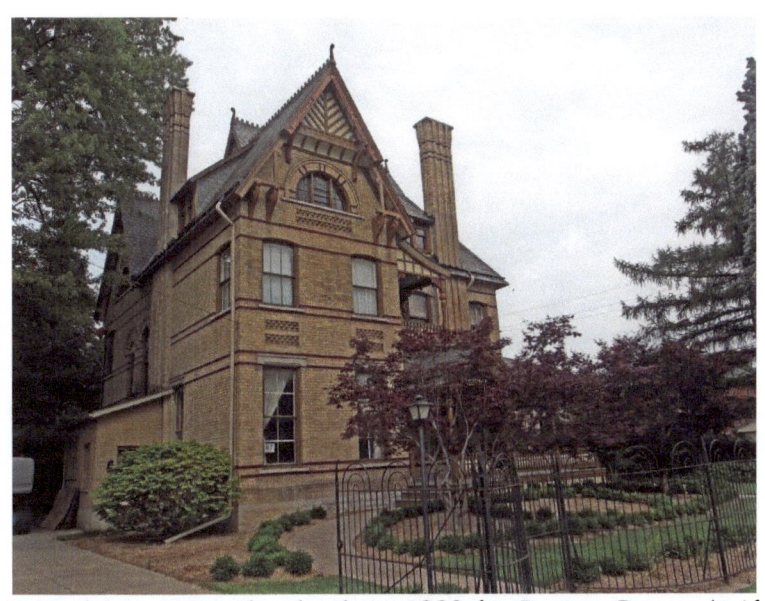

67 Peel Street South – built in 1883 for James Carter (wife Mary Box), only son of George Carter, a successful grain merchant in St. Marys – steep gable roofs, tall windows and chimneys with decorative brickwork – Queen Anne style - St Marys Book 2

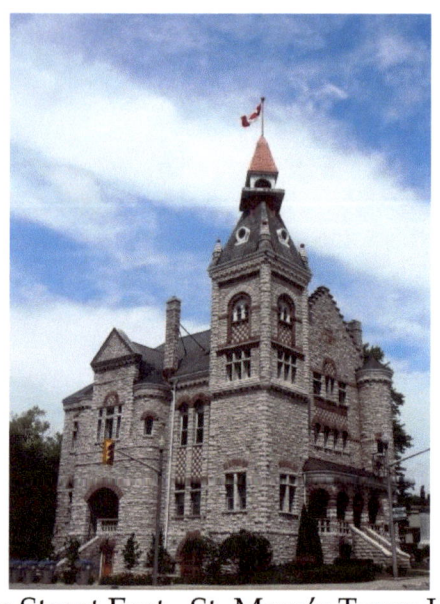

175 Queen Street East - St. Mary's Town Hall - This Romanesque Revival building was built in 1901 of local limestone with red sandstone as the contrasting elements for window arches and checkerboard effects in the façade. The massive entrances on the south and west façades of the building and the two towers on the south add to its lasting beauty. Due to its prominent location on the north side of the main street, and dominating as it does the sky-line of the Town, it plays an important role in the character of the downtown area.

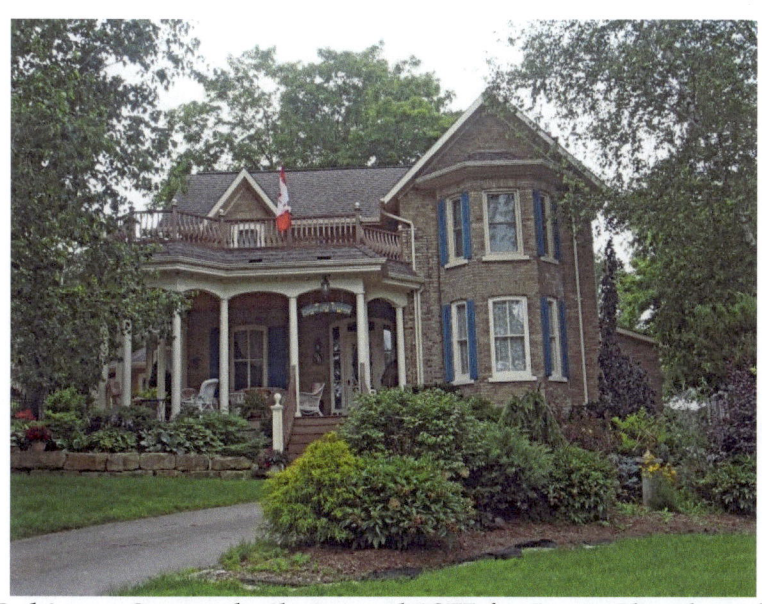

96 Robinson Street - built around 1875 for Leon Clench and his wife Eunice Cruttenden. It is now the Riverside Bed and Breakfast. Clench was a lawyer, a builder, inventor, violin-maker, musician and furniture-maker. Italianate style
- St Marys Book 3

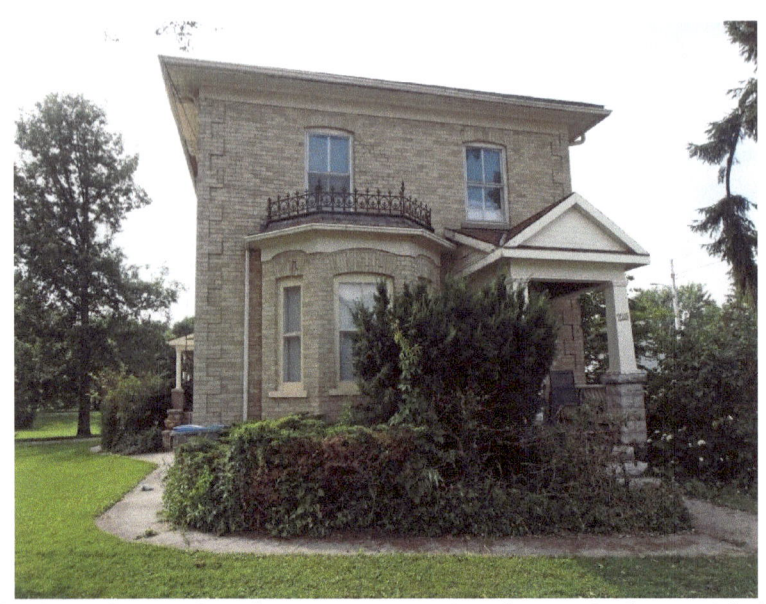

226 Water Street South – corner quoins, bay window with iron cresting above, pediment

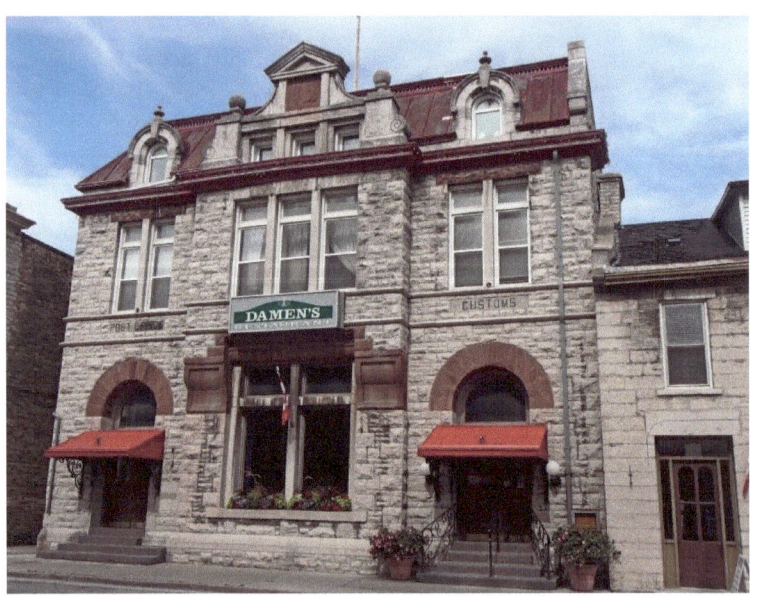

17 Water Street South – The Post Office and Customs House built in 1908 – Romanesque style

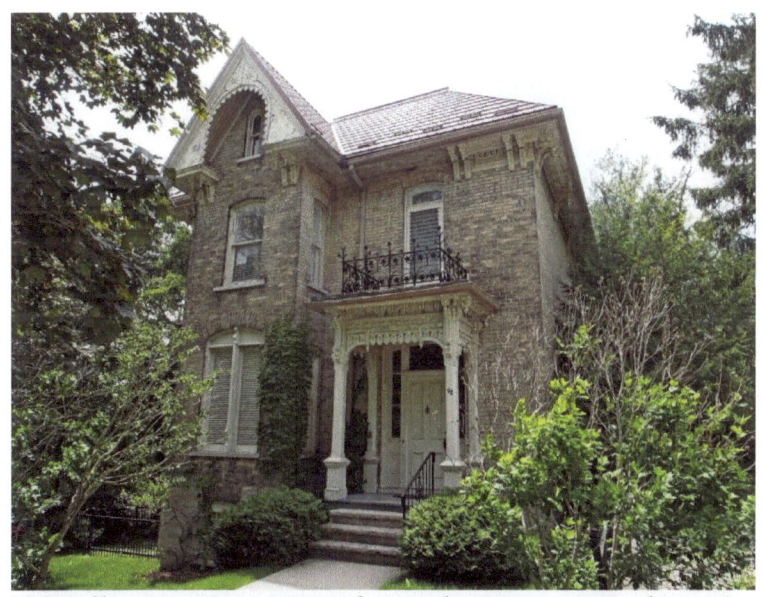

92 Wellington Street North – Italianate – paired cornice brackets, 2½ storey tower-like bay with verge board trim on gable, iron cresting above entrance porch - St Marys Book 4

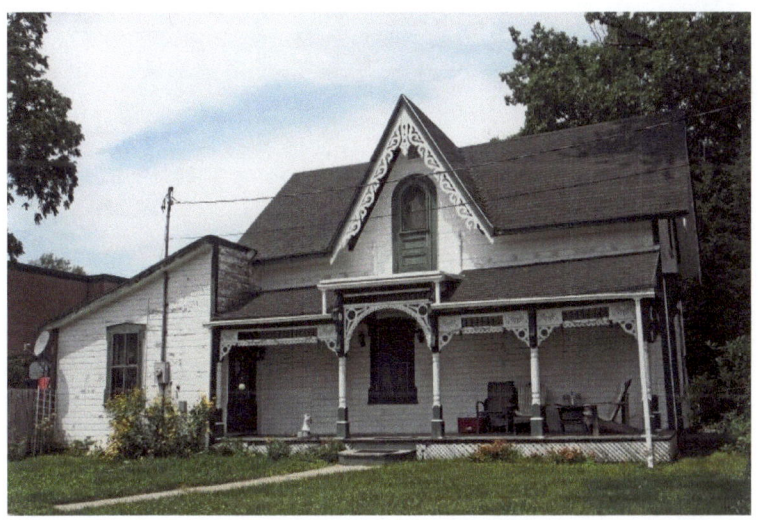

146 Wellington Street North – Gothic Revival, verge board trim on gable, bric-a-brac and stenciling on porch

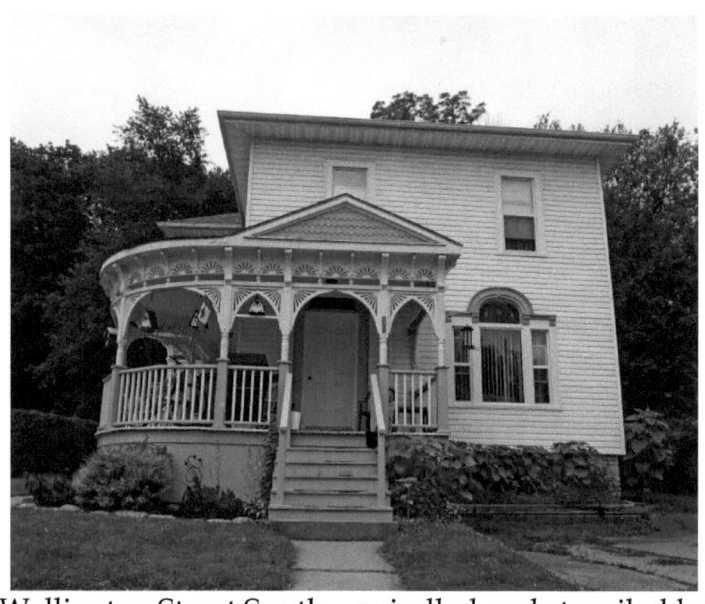

127 Wellington Street South – spindled and stenciled bric-a-brac on wraparound verandah; Palladian type window with window hood and stained glass window

Sarnia, Ontario – My Top 20 Picks

Sarnia is a city in Southwestern Ontario located on the eastern bank of the junction between the Upper and Lower Great Lakes where Lake Huron flows into the St. Clair River, which forms the Canada-United States border, directly across from Port Huron, Michigan. It is the largest city on Lake Huron. The city's natural harbor first attracted the French explorer LaSalle, who named the site "The Rapids" when he had horses and men pull his forty-five-ton barque "Le Griffon" up the almost four-knot current of the St. Clair River in August 1679. This was the first time anything other than a canoe or other oar-powered vessel had sailed into Lake Huron.

Captain Richard Emeric Vidal (1784-1854), one of the founders of Sarnia nurtured the little settlement for twenty years from his first visit in 1834. His wife, Charlotte Penrose Mitton (1790-1873) lived her last forty years in Sarnia and three streets bear her name (Charlotte, Penrose, and Mitton Streets).

Paul Blundy was born in Sarnia in 1918. He served in the Royal Canadian Navy in World War II. Following the war, he co-founded the McKenzie & Blundy Funeral Home. Paul served four years as a member of the Hydro-electric Commission, twenty years as a member of Sarnia City Council, eight of them as mayor. During his time on City Council, he was a strong advocate for the redevelopment of the waterfront. From 1977 to 1981, he served as M.P.P. for Sarnia. He died in 1992.

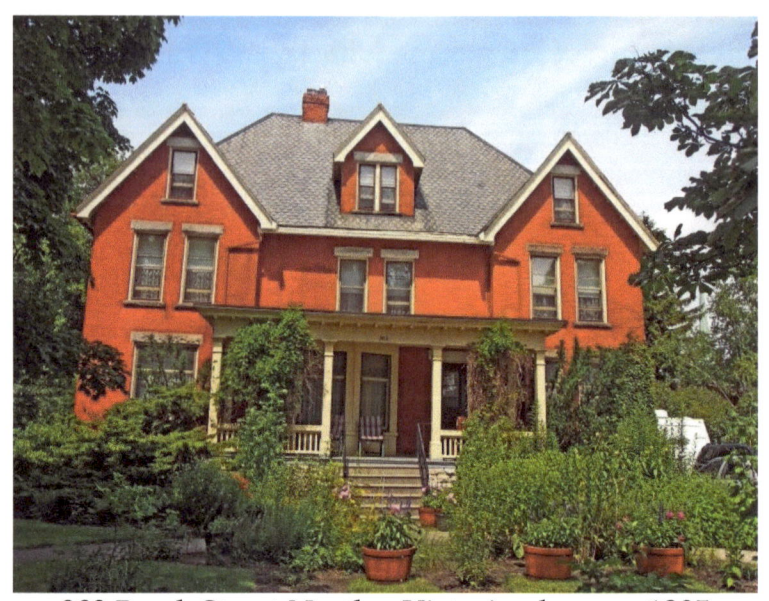

303 Brock Street North – Victorian home – 1895 – Sarnia Book 1

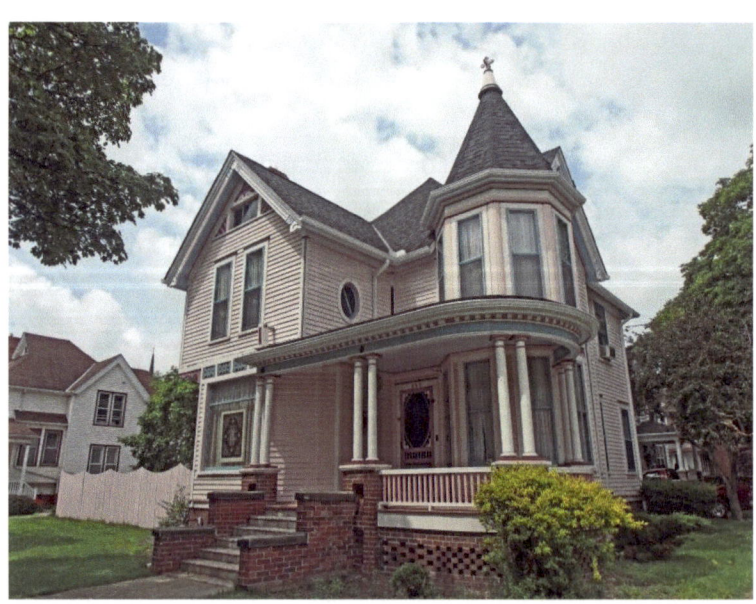

283 Brock Street North – 1900 – Queen Anne – turret, curved verandah

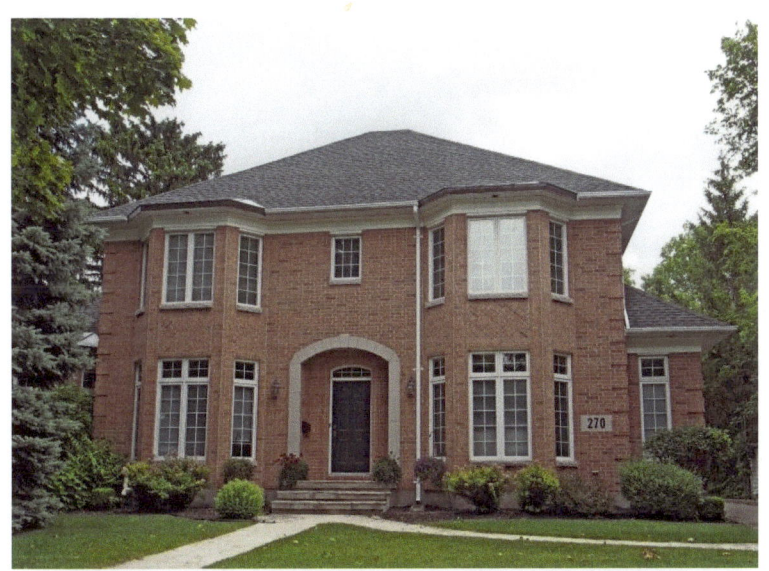

270 Brock Street North – 1890 - Georgian

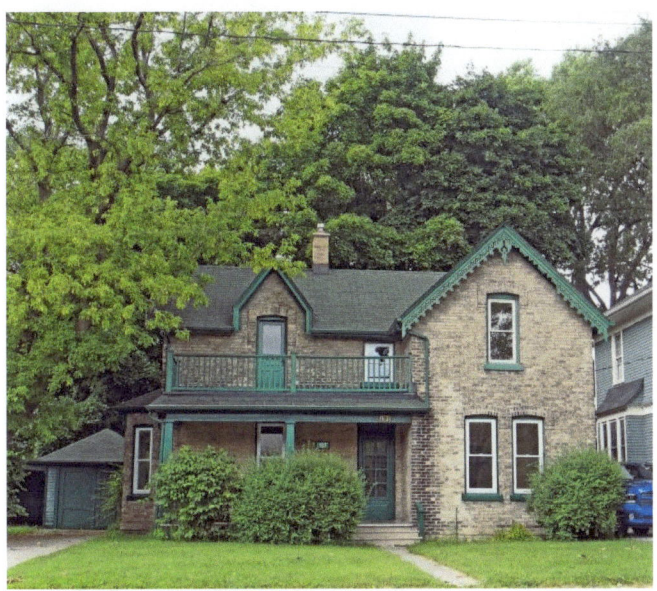

191 Brock Street South – Gothic Revival - 1890

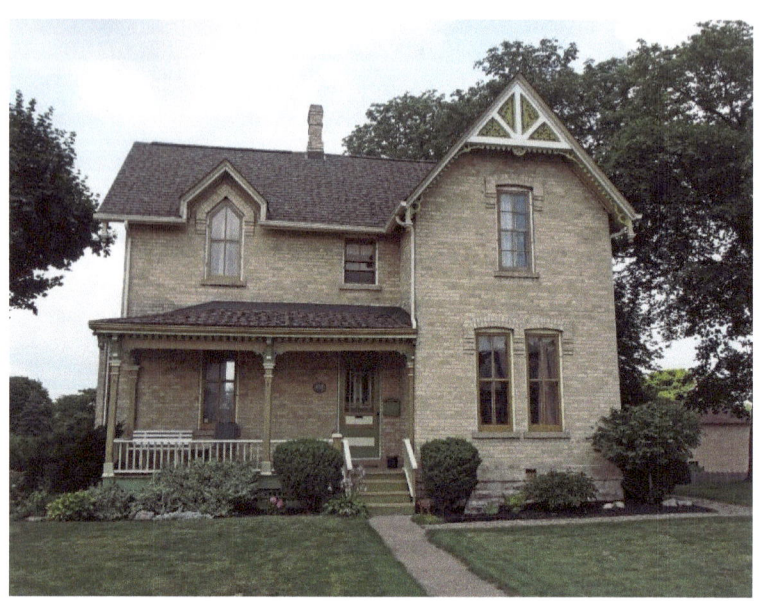

435 Christina Street North – 1890 – Gothic Revival – bargeboard trim on gable with stenciling, arched and rectangular windows with voussoirs

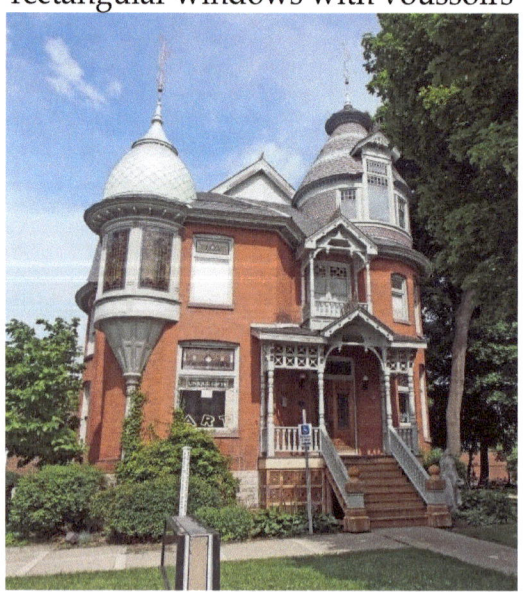

127 Christina Street South – Lawrence Family mansion – Mr. Lawrence was a lumberman – Queen Anne style – 1892

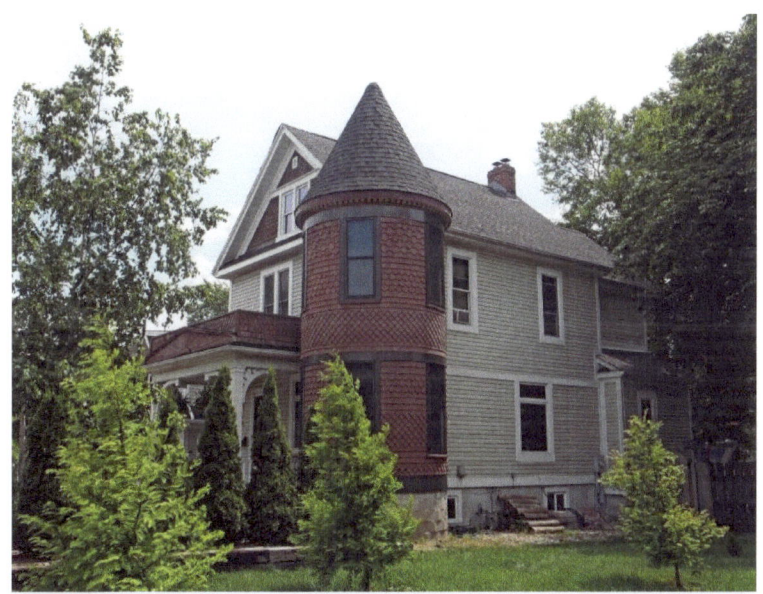

1031 Ellwood Avenue – 1890 – Edwardian – Sarnia Book 2

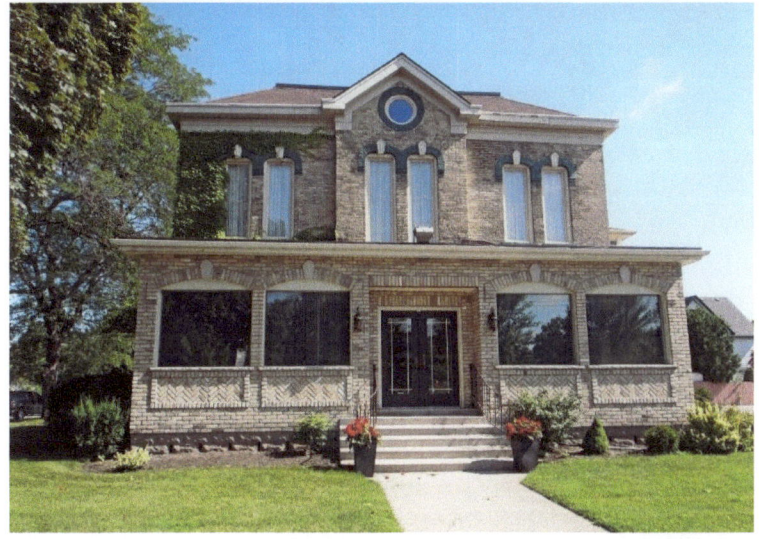

254 George Street – McCormack Funeral Home, Stewart Chapel – 1880 – Italianate - three bay two storey yellow brick building with a central frontispiece topped by a gable with projecting eaves; gable has a blinded round window; brick voussoirs over windows with carved oak leaf keystone; semi-elliptical brick arch doorway with a shared transom

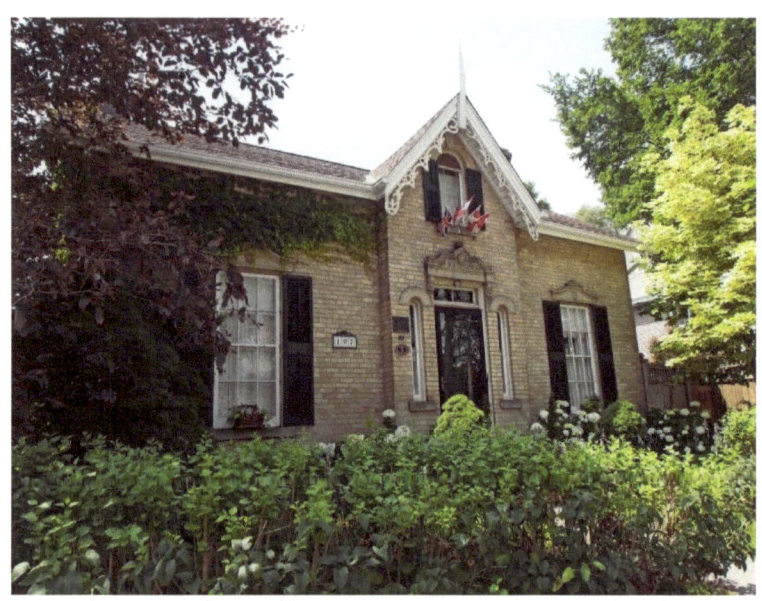

197 London Road, Mulberry House 1867 – Gothic/Georgian style - 1½ storey yellow brick home, stone foundation; centered on the façade is a frontispiece with a gable roof – Sarnia Book 3

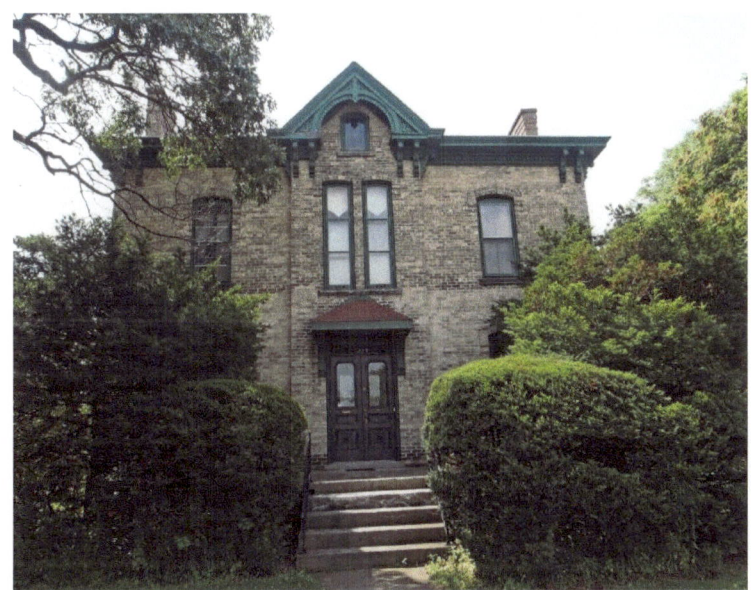

223 London Road – 1880 – Italianate - three bay, two storey yellow brick house with a centered frontispiece topped by a gable with a semi-circular arch decorated with bargeboard

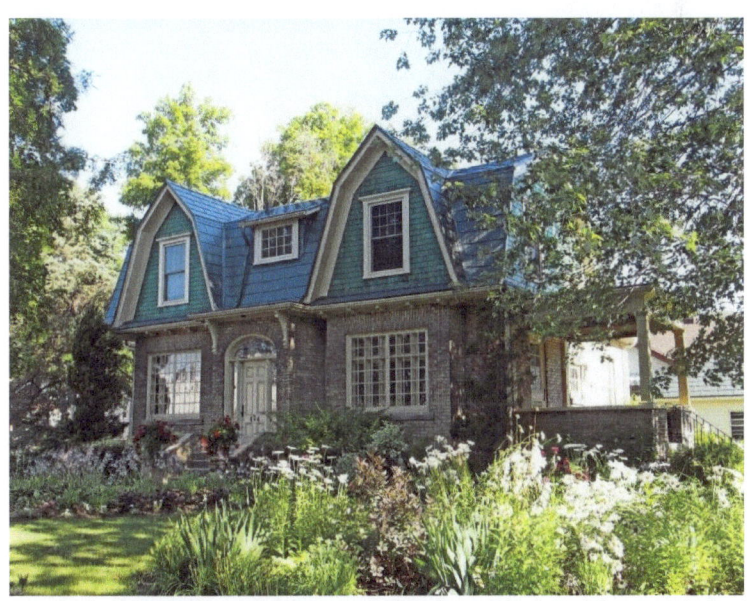

424 London Road – 1911 – gambrel roofed gables, sidelights and transom

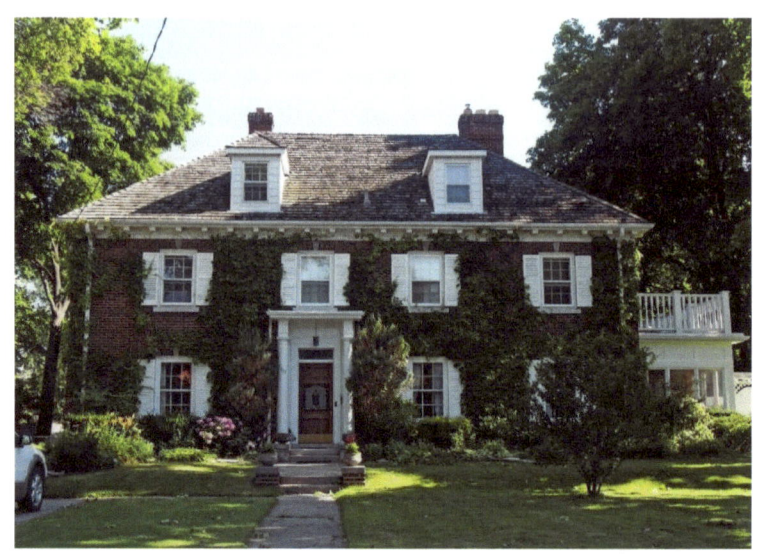

312 London Road – 1922 – Georgian – dormers, transom window

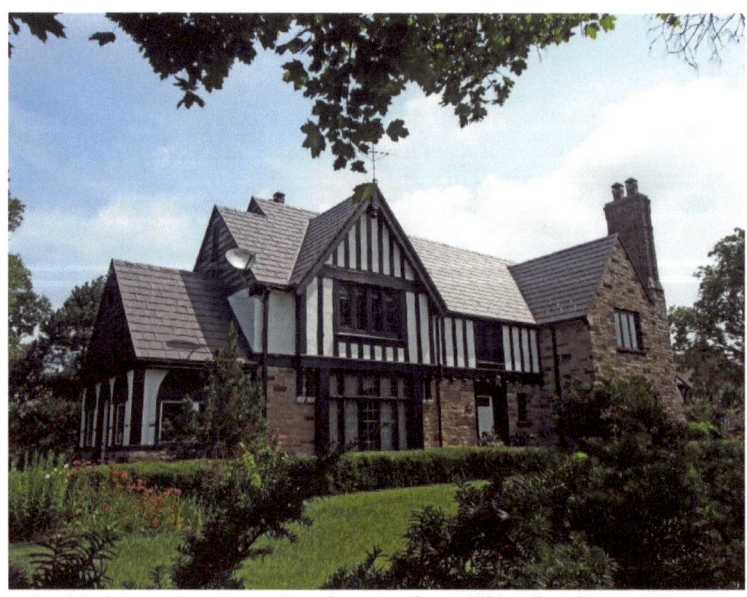

144 Maria Street – Tudor style – Elizabethan Manor

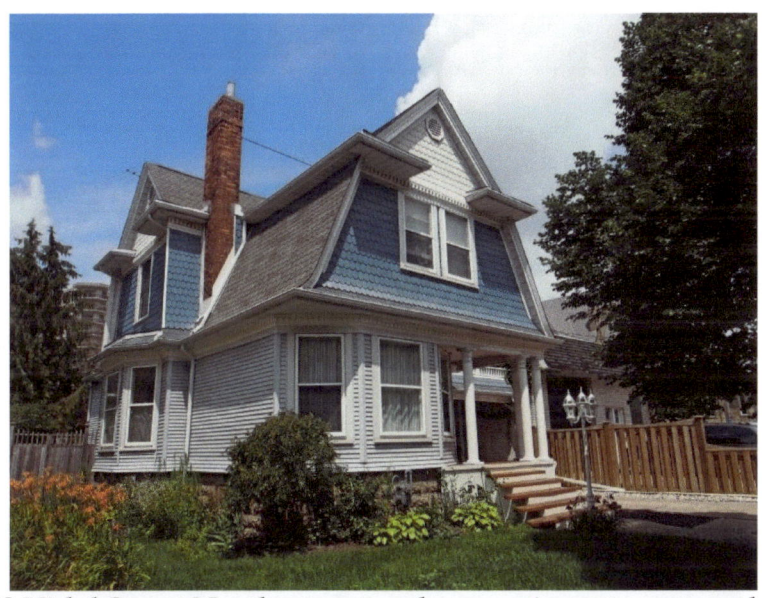

329 Vidal Street North – vernacular, cornice return on gable, wide cornice overhang, fish scale patterning, dentil molding – Sarnia Book 4

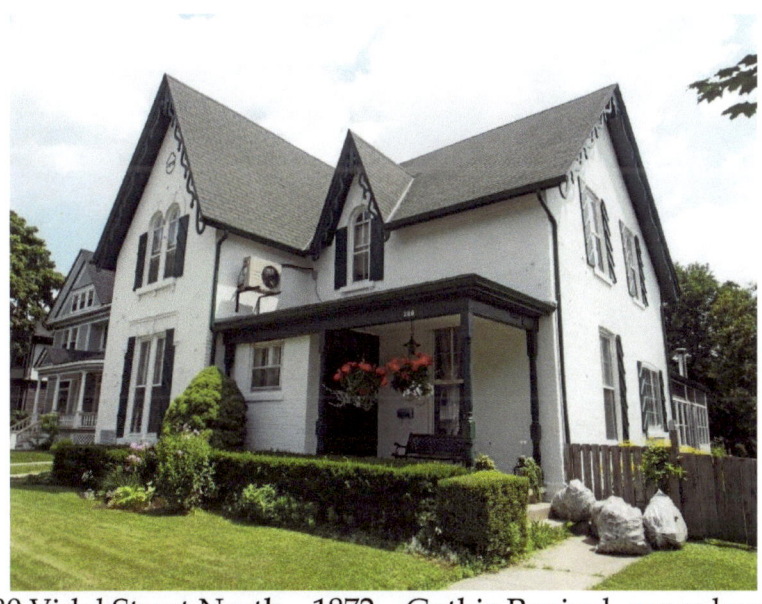

280 Vidal Street North – 1872 – Gothic Revival, verge board trim on gables, voussoirs with keystones

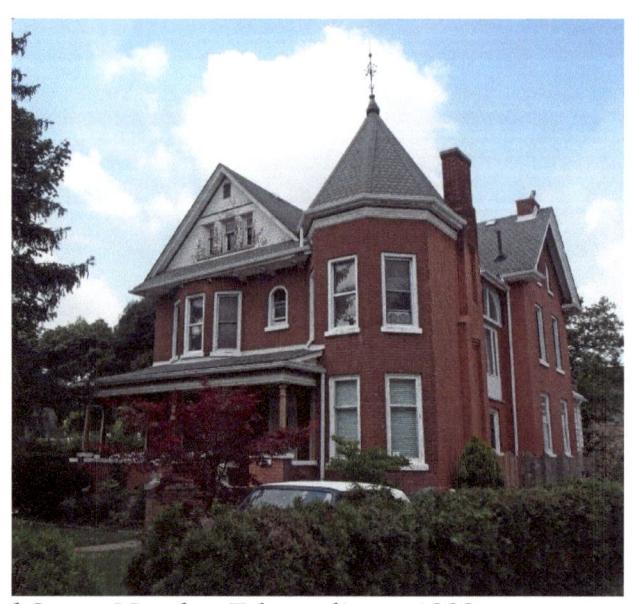

279 Vidal Street North – Edwardian – 1900 – two-storey tower with cone-shaped cap

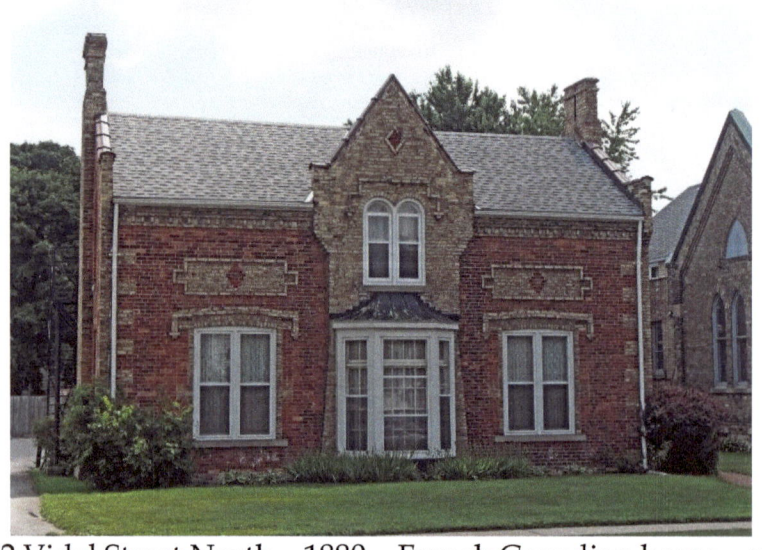

262 Vidal Street North – 1880 – French Canadian home – red and yellow brick detailing, gabled parapets, French bay window

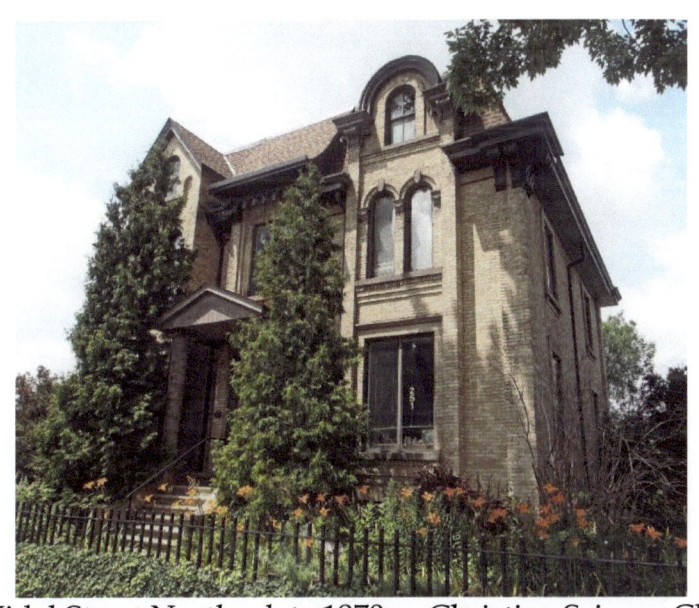

251 Vidal Street North – late 1870s – Christian Science Church – bell-cast mansard roof – Second Empire style, vousoirs and keystones, cornice brackets

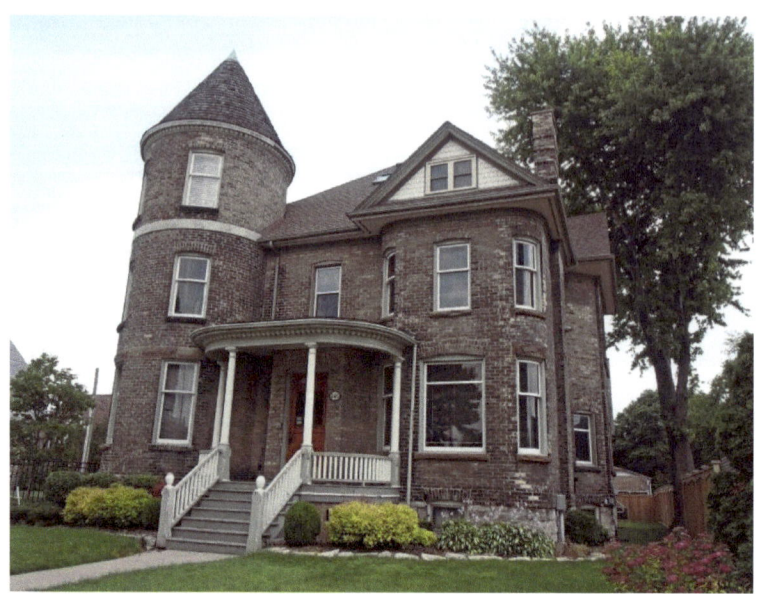

240 Vidal Street North – 1900 – Victorian - 3-storey tower with conical roof covered with cedar shingles, fish scale patterning in gable

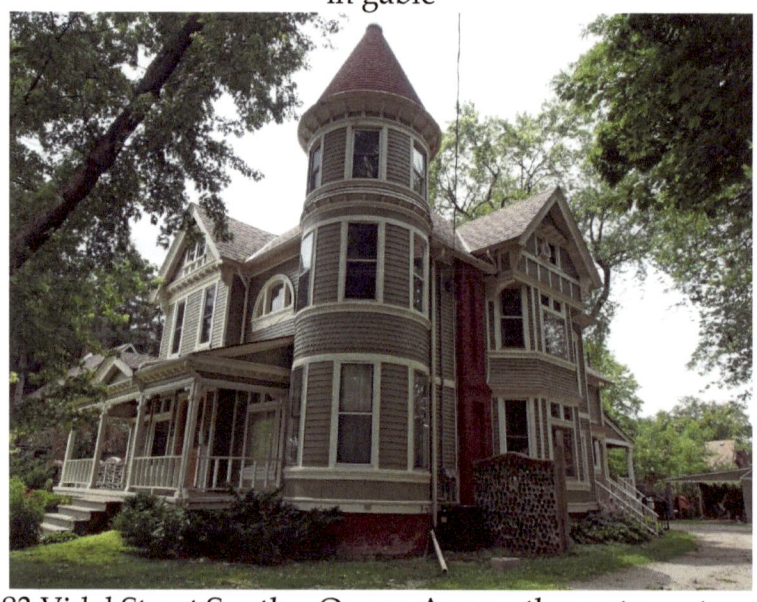

183 Vidal Street South – Queen Anne – three-storey turret with cone shaped roof

Petrolia, Ontario – My Top 7 Picks

Petrolia is a town in Ontario twenty minutes from Sarnia, and fifty minutes from London.

Following the discovery of oil at Oil Springs in 1857, prospectors extended their search to the entire township of Enniskillen. At the site of Petrolia, which contained two small settlements with post offices named Durance and Ennis, a well was brought into production in 1860. The following year a small refinery was opened and the Durance Post Office renamed "Petrolea". In 1865-66, the drilling of the King well established Petrolia as the major oil producing center in Canada and its population soared from about three hundred to two thousand three hundred.

Oil men from Petrolia travelled to the far reaches of the world (Gobi Desert, Arctic, Iran, Indonesia, the United States, Australia, Russia, and over eighty other countries) teaching others how to find and extract crude oil. Some oil fields in the area are still operational to this day.

Oil enticed people to come here, but Petrolia was created, nurtured, and sustained by hardworking visionaries, shopkeepers, builders, drillers, laborers, and leaders.

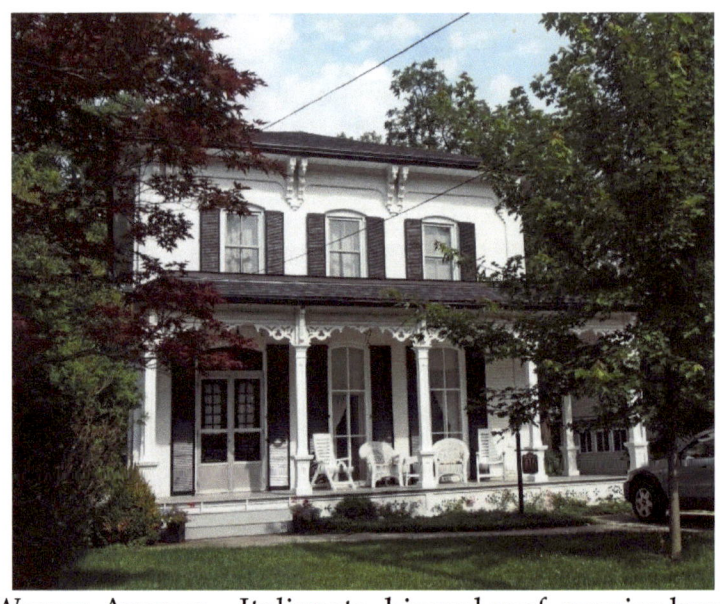

416 Warren Avenue – Italianate, hipped roof, cornice brackets, bric-a-brac on verandah

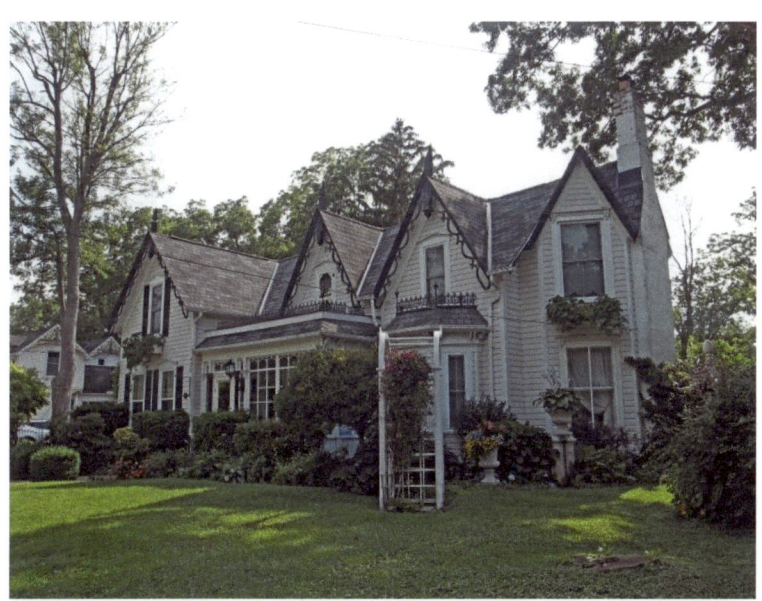

429 Ella Street – Lancey Hall built by Henry Warren Lancey – c. 1876 – Gothic Revival – verge board trim and finials on gables, iron cresting above bay window and enclosed front porch

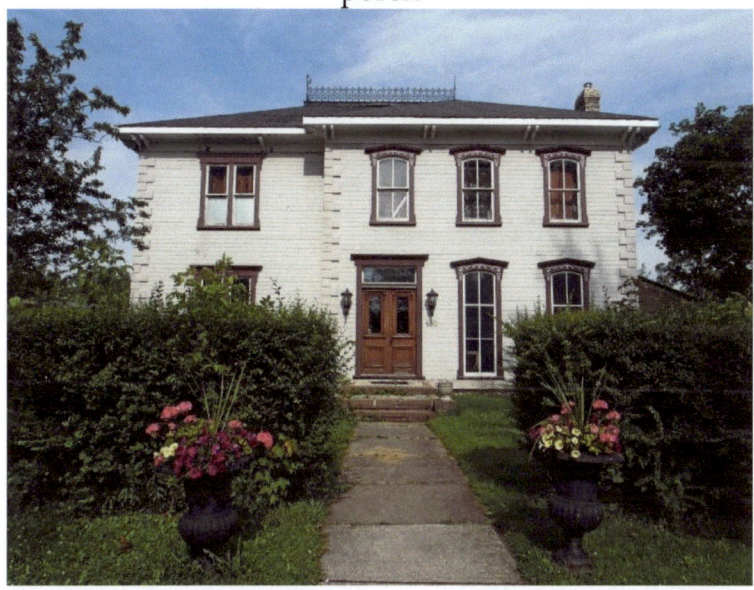

#430 – Italianate, hipped roof, corner quoins, iron cresting on roof (widow's walk), paired cornice brackets

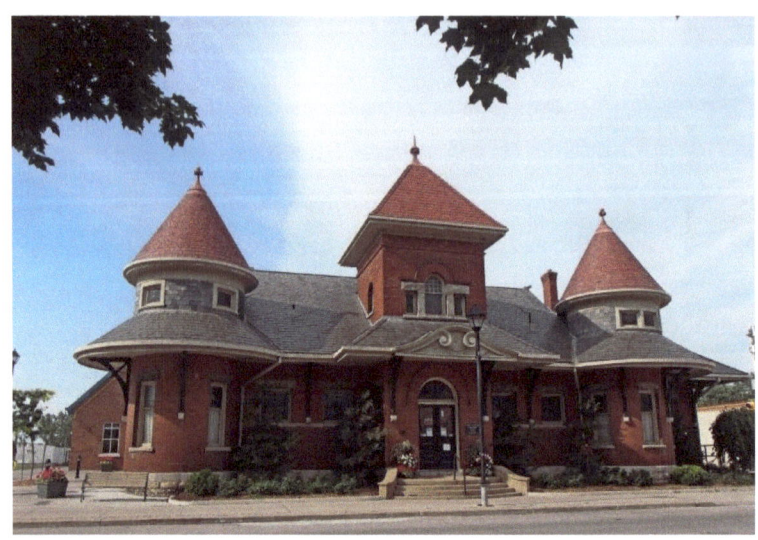

4200 Petrolia Line – The original Grand Trunk Railway Station was built in 1903. Designated heritage building now the Robert M. Nichol Library; turrets on each end, center tower

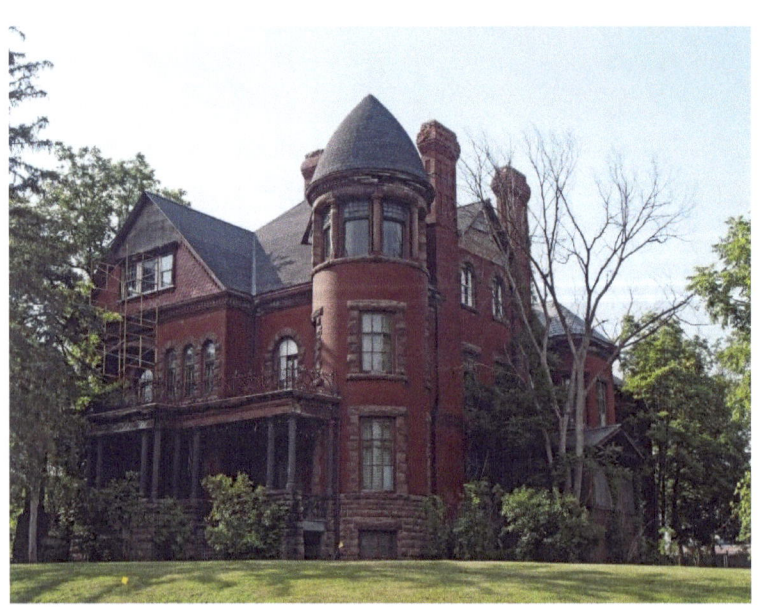

Petrolia Line – Romanesque, three-storey turret, decorative iron railing on second floor balcony

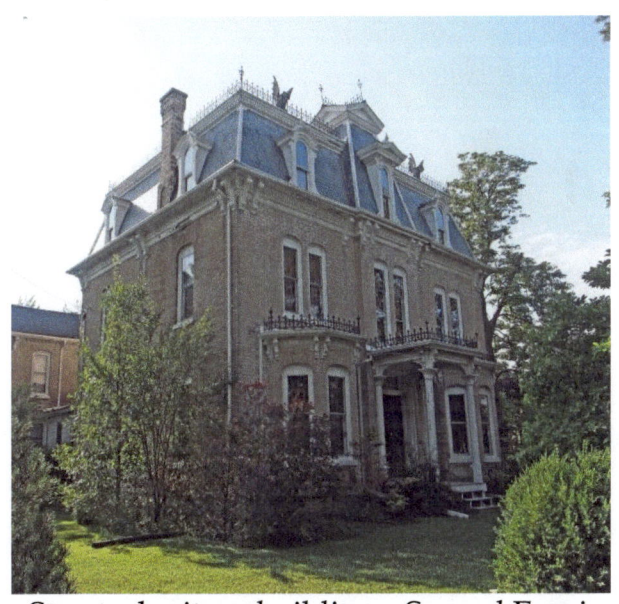

Queen Street – heritage building – Second Empire style, mansard roof, window hoods, iron cresting, cornice brackets, pillared entrance, bay windows

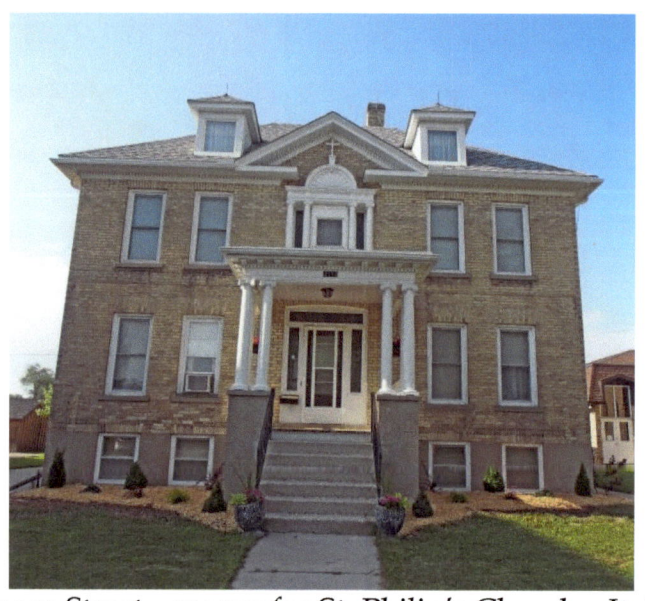

4142 Queen Street – manse for St. Philip's Church – Italianate, hipped roof, dormers, pillared entrance with Ionic capitals, dentil molding, sidelights and transom window

www.ingramcontent.com/pod-product-compliance
Lightning Source LLC
Chambersburg PA
CBHW040225220526
45473CB00001B/119